A Parent's Guide
to Online Safety

Doug Fodeman • Marje Monroe

HomePage Books

HomePage Books is an imprint of the
International Society for Technology in Education
EUGENE, OREGON • WASHINGTON, DC

A Parent's Guide to Online Safety

Doug Fodeman and Marje Monroe

Director of Book Publishing: *Courtney Burkholder*
Acquisitions Editor: *Jeff V. Bolkan*
Production Editors: *Lynda Gansel, Tina Wells*
Production Coordinator: *Emily Reed*
Graphic Designer: *Signe Landin*
Developmental Editor: *Tom Landon*
Copy Editor: *Janet Mehl*
Proofreader: *Ann Skaugset*
Cover Design: *Signe Landin*
Book Design and Production: *Kim McGovern*

Library of Congress Cataloging-in-Publication Data

Fodeman, Doug.
  A parent's guide to online safety / Doug Fodeman and Marje Monroe. — First edition.
     pages cm
  ISBN 978-1-56484-327-2
1. Internet and children—United States. 2. Internet in education—United States. 3. Internet—Security measures.
4. Internet—Safety measures. I. Monroe, Marje. II. Title.
  HQ784.I58F63 2013
  004.67'8083—dc23

                                                        2012047777

First Edition
ISBN: 978-1-56484-327-2 (paperback)
ISBN: 978-1-56484-470-5 (e-book)
Printed in the United States of America

Book Art: © istockphoto.com: laflor (cover); bowdenimages (pp. 1, 57, 63, 73, cover); svetikd (p. 5); monkeybusinessimages (p. 13, cover); Alina555 (p. 23); LattaPictures (p. 33, cover); shapecharge (p. 41, cover); anouchka (p. 47, cover).

ISTE® is a registered trademark of the International Society for Technology in Education.

About ISTE

The International Society for Technology in Education (ISTE) is the trusted source for professional development, knowledge generation, advocacy, and leadership for innovation. ISTE is the premier membership association for educators and education leaders engaged in improving teaching and learning by advancing the effective use of technology in PK–12 and teacher education.

Home to ISTE's annual conference and exposition and the widely adopted NETS, ISTE represents more than 100,000 professionals worldwide. We support our members with information, networking opportunities, and guidance as they face the challenge of transforming education. To find out more about these and other ISTE initiatives, visit our website at www.iste.org.

As part of our mission, ISTE Book Publishing works with experienced educators to develop and produce practical resources for classroom teachers, teacher educators, technology leaders, and parents. Every manuscript we select for publication is carefully peer-reviewed and professionally edited. We look for content that emphasizes the effective use of technology where it can make a difference—both at school and at home. We value your feedback on this book and other ISTE products. Email us at books@iste.org.

International Society for Technology in Education
Washington, DC, Office:
    1710 Rhode Island Ave. NW, Suite 900, Washington, DC 20036-3132
Eugene, Oregon, Office:
    180 West 8th Ave., Suite 300, Eugene, OR 97401-2916
Order Desk: 1.800.336.5191
Order Fax: 1.541.302.3778
Customer Service: orders@iste.org
Book Publishing: books@iste.org
Book Sales and Marketing: booksmarketing@iste.org
Web: www.iste.org

About the Authors

Since 1997, Marje Monroe and Doug Fodeman have worked with elementary, middle, and high schools throughout the country, helping teachers, administrators, parents, and children understand and cope with the many issues affecting children online. For many years they have conducted surveys and collected data concerning the behavior of children and teens online. They have published results of their data and many articles in a variety of newspapers and magazines. In addition, their 2009 book, *Racing to Keep Up: Talking with Your Kids about Technology Use and Ways to Keep the Home Computer Safe*, was published specifically as a resource for parents. Monroe and Fodeman's website, ChildrenOnline.org, supports their work with parents and schools. Parents and educators will find many valuable resources there, including a free monthly newsletter and blog.

 **Doug Fodeman** has been the director of technology at Brookwood School, a PK–8 school in Manchester, Massachusetts, since 1996. In addition, he taught high school science for 18 years, beginning in 1979, and served as director of technology at the Pingree School in South Hamilton, Massachusetts. He's given workshops on a wide variety of related topics, such as using search engines effectively, protecting privacy online, and telecollaboration. Fodeman has been a guest speaker on several radio shows, including WBZ in Boston and WLSAM in Chicago, and has appeared on the *CBS Evening News* and *ABC World News*, speaking about the topic of cell phone scams targeting children as well as other issues affecting children online.

 **Marje Monroe** is a clinical social worker and educator in schools, with close to 25 years of counseling, programming, and teaching experience. Formerly dean of students at Stoneleigh-Burnham School in Greenfield, Massachusetts, she has worked at five schools, including Buckingham Browne and Nichols School in Cambridge, Massachusetts, where she was director of counseling. She served as counselor and substance abuse coordinator at Wittenberg University in Springfield, Ohio, and as executive director of the Winnetka, Illinois, Youth Center. Throughout her career, Monroe has taught advanced placement psychology and English and has developed curricula for sex education, substance abuse, ethics, and decision making.

Contents

Contents

Technologies Change Quickly— I Can't Keep Up!

Trying to keep up with today's technology can be overwhelming. You probably feel like you'll never understand the technology your child is using, especially when it seems to change every six months. The MySpace of yesterday becomes the Facebook of today. Children and teens love to explore new online gadgets, gimmicks, games, and websites, and they often discover new and unexpected uses of these technologies. What's a parent to do?

Take a deep breath. Yes, the technology keeps changing, but the kids themselves stay pretty much the same. Much of what they do is not about the technology they are using. It's about seeking attention, forming and sustaining relationships, taking risks, and having fun. Parents have been dealing with these behaviors for centuries—your own parents probably dealt with you behaving this way when you were young.

Look beyond the new gadget, website, or technological tool, and try to understand the activity your child is engaging in while using the technology. You don't need to panic in the face of new devices, once you realize that the technology is just the latest forum for kids to reach out to others, form identities, and push boundaries.

Some Principles Always Apply

One of our biggest jobs as parents is to set limits according to kids' developmental levels throughout their lives. Childproof latches, for example, stop toddlers from exploring kitchen cabinets. We hold hands with a 5-year-old when crossing the street, and we follow our 10-year-old to the park when he rides his bike there for the first time.

Try to view technology in the same way. If your 10-year-old wants to broadcast herself online from her bedroom, ask yourself if she is ready to face the risks of that sort of public exposure, where anyone watching might try to contact her. As in every situation, when your child is using technology, your goal should be to look at the issues facing your child and set boundaries based on that child's developmental level.

You Are the Adult

Being a parent in a world with so much new technology is challenging. It's your job to stay vigilant, to understand all the risks, and to warn your child effectively about potential dangers, especially when the landscape keeps shifting. However, keep in mind that you have been guiding your child since infancy. You are the adult—the keeper of your family's values—and you already know what to do.

When faced with new and unfamiliar technological influences, it's okay to tell your child that you need to better understand the risks regarding those technologies before he uses them. Once you understand the issues, consider whether or not the innovation is developmentally healthy for your child. In other words, is your child prepared to deal with the issues it presents?

Should your 7-year-old, for example, be allowed to chat with others unsupervised on Club Penguin? The answer to that question should be based on your assessment of whether she is able to discriminate between online friends and others who may treat her badly. Can your 7-year-old make thoughtful decisions before acting and be nice online while playing a game? Is she ready to ignore or properly deal with the hurtful language that is common in online communications? Probably not, but you have to be the final judge of what your own child can handle.

ChildrenOnline.org: Who We Are

We are Doug Fodeman and Marje Monroe, and we are experts in technology and online safety, counseling, and education. Through our website, ChildrenOnline.org, we provide parents and schools with practical, real-life solutions to the issues faced by young people using technology. Since 1997, we have spoken to thousands of students, parents, and teachers.

In addition to the many tools and resources we provide on our website, we offer innovative and comprehensive workshops on online safety and education to students, parents, faculty, and administrators. Our approach, unique in the field of Internet safety, combines a thorough understanding of Internet technologies, child development, and counseling.

Each year, we survey two thousand to three thousand students in Grades 4 through 12. Students are asked questions about their online activities and attitudes. You will see some of the results of our 2011 survey in the chapters that follow.

Students who took the survey are described as being at various grade levels, rather than as being at various ages. There are two reasons for presenting the data in this way. First, the data were collected in schools by grade level, and second, we have observed over the years that peer influences in grade levels within schools can have a tremendous impact on behavior. This means behaviors tend to spread rapidly across a grade level regardless of the ages of the students in that grade.

Because we sample only at the schools we visit, the sampling doesn't equally represent every socioeconomic level or all ethnic populations across the United States. Even so, we are sure you will find it interesting. And while it may be anecdotal, the data coming from public school students is consistent with the data provided by independent school students. We have little reason to believe that our data would vary significantly from that of a broader population of students.

You Can Do It!

Different families have different rules, but fundamentally, all parents create rules to help their children grow up in healthy and developmentally appropriate ways. There are no rules or boundaries built into the online world, so you must define your child's limits there, too.

You have been a parent for years, imparting values, making difficult decisions, and setting boundaries for your child. Take some time to think through how you can translate these skills to the ever-changing sea of technology. Talk to your child, ask questions, research the issues involved, and be a presence in your child's online world. Don't assume that just because he *can* use a technology that he *should* use it. Take heart, take a deep breath, and make good decisions. You have been doing that for years!

CHAPTER 1

How Old
Is Old Enough?

There are many guideposts for parents trying to raise physically and emotionally healthy children. Movie ratings, ratings on video games, driving rules, and minimum age limits for alcohol consumption are some examples. However, when it comes to dealing with technology use, parents are often left with little or no guidance. Our hope is to create some simple and clear guide-posts to help you steer your child safely through her technology use.

Setting Boundaries

You already know how to set boundaries:

> "Stop hitting your brother."

> "No, you may not have another cookie."

> "Stay away from the ledge."

> "Call me once you get to your friend's house."

> "You may watch only PG movies."

> "No, you may not take the car tonight. Your father will drive you."

Every day we set rules and limits for our children, and almost as often children push against those boundaries. Some of the limits we set seem automatic to us. Teaching kids to share toys, to be kind, to go to bed on time, to eat their vegetables, and to look both ways seems almost instinctual. We have experienced each of those things ourselves—we remember our own parents guiding us on these matters.

Most of us didn't grow up texting, instant messaging, socializing online, or being connected to a smartphone for much of the day. We don't have memories to fall back on, and so we are forced to invent ways to parent our kids online. In this ever-changing world of technology, we have to deal with cyberbullying, Facebook, texting, live multiplayer gaming, instant messaging, anonymous online communication, and the ability of anyone, anywhere to reach out to our children (and the reverse).

The good news is this: If we follow the age-old practice of creating rules based on children's developmental stages, it is not hard to apply those same rules to technology.

Recommended Grade Levels for Technology Use

These are the grade levels and ages at which children are typically developmentally ready to handle the risks presented by the technology listed. Your child may not be typical. To make the decision that is best for your child, examine the technology and gauge your child's ability to cope with its challenges.

- **Before about the fourth grade (age 9):** Children should have limited, supervised access to the Internet.

- **About sixth grade (age 11):** Start allowing chatting or the use of instant messaging.

- **About ninth grade (age 14):** Start allowing texting.

- **About tenth grade (age 15):** Start allowing membership on social networking sites.

- **Until eleventh grade (age 16):** You should have full login access to all of your child's online accounts and you should log into your child's accounts routinely. (Please note: "Friending" your child is very different from having password access to your child's account. As a "friend," your child can easily hide content from you in social networks.)

Let Child Development Be Your Guide

When your 5-year-old asks to watch a PG-13 movie, you probably instantly say "no," understanding that there will likely be content beyond the understanding of your child. Just as a PG-13 movie is likely beyond a 5-year-old's intellectual and emotional capacity, so is chatting online or playing online games with a social component such as Webkinz or Club Penguin. When we say "social component," that means that part of the game involves the ability to send messages to and receive messages from other players while playing. Small children might face material that is inappropriate for them at these

Create a Healthy Balance

Here are some broad suggestions that will make your child's free time more balanced and his computer use sensible and safe.

- Maintain a healthy balance in your child's play. Include plenty of time for friends, family, or solitary offline play. Encourage group sports and family events.

- Consider putting parental control software on the family computer when your child is young. With this software in place, your child will grow up understanding the jurisdiction that you have over his exploration of the Internet. As he matures, it will always be easier to remove limits than to add new boundaries that didn't previously exist.

- Any computer your child uses should be placed in a common, easily visible, or high-traffic area of your home, where it is easy to supervise usage. Set clear time allowances and curfews for using the Internet. Hold off on wireless Internet access via laptops, iPads, iPod Touch, smartphones, and other devices until your child is in high school. Even then, set limits and curfews on technology use.

- Spend time going over your child's favorite sites—alone and then with your child. Create rules and structures for your child's time on the sites.

- Include values and ethics when talking about the Internet. Encourage children to act the same online as they do in person, and to be kind and respectful. A great deal of the language and communication online is harassing, mean, and inappropriate. Your child should understand that such communication goes against your family's values.

- Encourage your child to talk to an adult whenever she feels frightened or uncomfortable about something she encounters online. Children often worry that their families will take away computer privileges if they report a problem.

- When purchasing a cell phone for your child, resist her request for a smartphone or one with texting capability until she reaches 14 or 15 years old.

websites. At the very least, children of this age should be supervised when using sites like these where they can interact with strangers.

When your 10-year-old asks to go to the mall with a group of friends without an adult, you would probably say "no," understanding that a group of 10-year-olds alone in a shopping mall might face situations that are beyond their abilities to handle—and the temptation to get into trouble might be a little too great as well. Similarly, most 10-year-olds are not yet ready to face the responsibilities and challenges associated with chatting or instant messaging online, or texting. With these forms of instantaneous communications, it is much too easy for a 10-year-old to bully or be bullied, to use or be exposed to inappropriate language, or to be tempted to engage in anonymous online communications.

Your 13-year-old begging to attend a high school party would probably be met with a "no" from you, since most 13-year-olds are not ready to make healthy decisions for themselves in the face of the peer pressure they are likely to feel in that situation. The same is true of social networking sites. Conversations on sites such as Facebook and Instagram may contain bullying, meanness, foul language, and comments about sexual situations, drugs, and alcohol. Developmentally, a 13-year-old is not ready to read or participate in these conversations.

Most owners of online sites for children are driven by profit, not child development. For example, the website Webkinz aims its advertising at young children and sells cute stuffed animals in malls all over the country. The stuffed animals include codes that can be redeemed on the website to get a prize. What 5-year-old doesn't love a cute stuffed animal?

Many social networking sites, including YouTube and Instagram, have set their minimum age requirement at 13 (and many kids lie about their age to gain access earlier). What is the reason that users are asked to wait until age 13? It's not because experts in childhood development have determined that age is the most appropriate age for children to begin using these online tools. Age 13 is simply the age at which the Children's Online Privacy Protection Act (COPPA) of 1998 allows children to sign up for online accounts and provide personal information without parental consent.

Skills Needed for Face-to-Face Conversations

Many children and teens turn to electronic communications to avoid having difficult face-to-face conversations. It is easier, for example, to break up with a boyfriend or girlfriend via texting or chat than it is to do it in person. Their friend may be hurt just as much or more by a text-message breakup, but delivering the message remotely allows the sender to avoid having to feel the hurt or see the tears.

Empathy is a skill that is not easily learned through online communication. With children turning to telecommunications at younger and younger ages and spending more and more time online, they may be losing out on the development of very important social skills that come from difficult face-to-face conversations. Learning to read cues from vocal intonations, facial expressions, and body language cannot be done online, yet they are necessary skills to have in an adult world. Empathy is learned by seeing the reactions of others.

Set limits to your child's time spent online. Encourage your child to spend face-to-face time with friends. Sherry Turkle, author of the 2011 book *Alone Together: Why We Expect More from Technology and Less from Each Other*, suggests that you encourage face-to-face conversation at home by creating no-texting zones. Consider insisting that your child (and you) not text in the kitchen and dining room—that those parts of the home are reserved for real conversations. Turkle also suggests that there be no texting allowed in the car on the way to or from school. That car time can be an especially good opportunity for you to talk with your child every school day.

Although we have a cultural understanding of raising kids in the physical world, many parents are in the dark when it comes to understanding life online. It is easy to see the risks associated with driving, sexual activity, drinking, and unsupervised parties. It is much harder to see into the murky world of the Internet. Children and teens can grow up faster via the Internet than is healthy or developmentally appropriate. The beguiling anonymity of a screen in a home can tempt children and teens to take risks and behave in ways they would never consider in their physical world—and can tempt parents into a false sense of security.

The solution? Apply the same boundaries to your child's technology activities that you do to the rest of his activities.

CHAPTER 2

Important Conversations

It is important to be aware of our children's activities, but sometimes there is such a gap between our children's online activities and our own online experiences that we don't even know what it is that we need to know. For example, who would think to ask an 11-year-old if he has uploaded videos of himself or his friends to YouTube or Instagram? Yet our 2010 research shows that nearly one out of every five (19%) sixth graders had done just that. An eighth grader should know better than to share her passwords for online accounts with friends, right? Our research shows that nearly half (46.6%) have shared a password. Our research also showed that, overall, students who shared a password were two-and-a-half times more likely to have their online accounts used (and misused) without their permission than were students who had not shared a password.

This chapter will suggest some questions to ask your child about life online, as well as offering some guidance. Obviously not all questions apply to all age levels. However, we recently heard from fifth graders who told us that they knew first and third graders with Facebook accounts, so it may be useful to ask younger children some questions that would reveal such behaviors.

The Introductory Conversation

Your child's online world might include hundreds of people she's accepted as "friends" on social networks; a presence on gaming sites; near-constant communication with friends and strangers via instant messaging, chat, text, and videoconferencing; and multiple email accounts. Although older children may protest and tell us that their lives online are none of our business, their safety and healthy development is, in fact, our business. As a parent, you have a fundamental responsibility to understand and monitor your child's behavior online, just as you try to understand and monitor her behavior in the physical world. The first step is sitting down with her to begin a conversation.

Preface your initial conversation with an explanation: You want to understand how your child is spending her time online. Go ahead and admit that you're naive about some of the technology and that you want her help in order to become more familiar with the parts of the online world she is enjoying.

Here are some questions you can ask to begin conversations with your child:

- What are your favorite websites? (If you feel you are not getting the entire story, open your child's web browser and review the browser's history. Deleted histories can be indicative of a child trying to hide his Internet behavior.)

- What online accounts have you signed up for?

- What email accounts do you have?

- Do you have instant messaging accounts?

- Have you used video chat? (iChat, Skype)

- Do you have a blog or vlog (video blog)?

- What gaming sites have you signed up for? Do you play Minecraft?

- Do you have any social network accounts? (Facebook, Tumblr, MySpace, Twitter, Instagram, or Formspring, for example)?

- Have you ever posted photos or videos online?

- Have you ever filled out surveys or quizzes online? Have you ever given personal information?

- Do you have friends online whom you don't know in person?

- Have you ever shared your password with friends? (If so, change that password!)

- Have friends ever texted you after you've gone to bed?

- Can you get on the Internet from your iPod or cell phone?

If your child has a Facebook account, you may also want to ask the following questions:

- How many Facebook friends do you have?

- Are any of those friends people you've never actually met?

- Have you visited the privacy and account settings lately to make sure they are what you want them to be? (Facebook privacy and account settings should be checked every month. The language of these settings is very misleading and difficult to understand.)

- Are you using any apps with your account? (If so, you may want to ask your children to show you the apps and see what permissions they have given the apps. Many apps misuse user information, and some are forms of malware.)

Using these questions as a starting point, you can better understand the scope of your child's online world, and you give the message that you are invested and interested in that part of her life.

Learn More

After your introductory conversation, spend some time online and ask yourself some questions. Go to each website that your child enjoys and see what's there. In some cases, you'll need to join the site to look around in any serious way. Note the information required when you join, because the site got the same sort of information from your child. Some sites require only an email address to join, but other sites are much more intrusive. Read the privacy policy.

If the site is designed for children, there will probably be information for parents. Read that information with a critical eye, because it is in the website's best interests to assure you that the site will be safe and possibly educational for your child. Does your gut tell you that the website's producers have good intentions? Have they designed the site in a way that matches their good intentions?

Is there advertising? If so, is it for other aspects of the website (or aspects of the company that controls the website), or is it for third-party products or services? Is the advertising appropriate to your child's developmental stage, and will your child understand that it is advertising? Ads are often disguised to be mini-games, surveys, or quizzes that trick children into giving away lots of personal information. Are you comfortable with the type of advertising? You can tell a lot about the character of the people running a website from the character of the advertising that they are willing to display. Try reloading the pages of a website several times to see what ads appear.

Look for other people's opinions about the website. Common Sense Media (www.commonsensemedia.org) is a great site for parents, with lists of websites, video games, and movies, including opinions on age-appropriateness. Wikipedia has good capsule summaries of nearly every significant social or gaming website, including criticisms that have been leveled at those sites in the past or present. Because of the user-written nature of Wikipedia, some of those descriptions contain bias (often because part of a description may have been supplied by someone with an economic interest in a particular website).

Fortunately, users of Wikipedia typically are diligent about prominently noting article bias and flagging questionable entries.

If anything you learn from your research about any of the websites makes you uncomfortable, use the specifics to formulate search engine searches to see if other people share your concerns. They probably do.

If your child has a cell phone or smartphone, look at your billing statement (you can usually go online to get a detailed billing statement). Your child's perception of his own phone use probably won't match the data from the phone company. Kids don't usually have any idea how much they really use their phones, any more than they can tell you how many times they touched their face with their hand yesterday. The detailed bill will tell you exactly how much (and when) they're using the phone. If they're using it too much or at inappropriate times, the phone company data will help you with the next conversation you need to have. All of today's major cell phone carriers offer some form of parental controls for children's accounts. Contact your carrier to inquire about the details.

Don't Forget to Be a Parent

Sometimes we parents forget the obvious, or need support ourselves, when we are making tough decisions. We would like to remind you of the following:

- It is okay to say "no" when you are unsure whether or not your child is ready for a particular technology or if you are unsure of the risks associated with using a technology. Your child can wait while you examine the issue.

- It is okay to change your mind, and the rules, once you've learned more about a technology, or if you aren't pleased with how your child is using a technology.

- Your children may know how to use technology, but they don't know how to parent themselves. That's your job—your most important job!

Continued

- No one else is looking out for your child online. That is your job. If you don't set appropriate boundaries, no one will.

- Just because children *can* use a technology doesn't mean they *should* use it—or that it is healthy or appropriate for them.

- It is not okay for your children to lie about their ages so they can sign up for online accounts.

- You know what is best for your child, and you set your family values.

- No matter how savvy our children may be using technology, they are still children, and children, even teenagers, are easily manipulated online.

As parents, we often feel that we will damage our children's social lives if we don't let them do what every other child seems to be doing. Many parents feel this way! Speak to other parents. They can be your strongest allies in raising healthy children in an age-appropriate manner. Try to find common ground. Imagine the power you will feel if a handful of parents of sixth-grade friends, for example, could agree upon a common set of rules and boundaries for all of their children. It might become a movement!

Recently, at a school where we presented workshops, one mother mentioned that she collected all cell phones at the door when her 12-year-old had friends over, including not allowing phones in the bedroom during sleepovers, despite the objection of her children and their friends. In just a few days, other mothers heard of this and called to tell her they loved the idea and were going to do the same thing!

The Follow-Up Conversation

So you've asked your child about his passwords and online friends, looked at your child's favorite websites, looked at the sites' privacy policies and advertising environments, and determined how and when he's using his phone. You now have the information you need to plan the next conversation with him. Combine what you've learned with your knowledge of your child's personality and maturity level, and use that to establish guidelines that suit your own style of parenting. Be clear and confident about what the rules are.

We're assuming that these are the first in-depth conversations that you and your child have had about his online world, and that you will establish guidelines based on what you've learned. If you have already established guidelines for online behavior and your introductory conversation revealed that rules are being broken, deal with that disobedience the way you deal with any other rule-breaking in your family.

Whatever you've decided to do, when you speak with your child again, you should cover these four areas:

1. Lay out your expectations for his future online behavior.

2. Explain the rules you've established to ensure that those expectations are met. Your rules will likely define new limits or boundaries around your child's use of technology.

3. Describe how you will monitor his compliance with the rules. (This is where parental control software or cell phone plans can be very helpful.)

4. Be clear and specific about what will happen if the rules are broken.

Don't try to make this up as you go along. Think long and hard about what you plan to say for all four points. Be open to discussion, consider arguments that your child might offer, and know how you plan to counter those arguments. Decide ahead of time what is negotiable and what is not.

Strategies to Consider

Here are some examples of strategies, rules, and expectations that work well for many families. You can adjust them to match your child's age and needs.

- Purchase and use parental-control software for home computers, tablets, and cell phones to help you set boundaries and monitor behavior. (See the Tools and Resources section at the end of this book.)

- Collect all smartphones, iPads, iPod Touches, and personal gaming devices overnight. This helps create non-Internet time at night to encourage sleep rather than late-night web browsing or game playing.

- Ask for the passwords for your child's online accounts, including gaming, social networking, video-chat, YouTube, and instant messaging sites. Check the sites regularly to ensure your child is behaving online according to your expectations.

- Routinely check your child's web browser history (the list of sites recently visited).

- Take all cell phones at the door when having groups of kids in your home. This is especially true at sleepovers. Most cell phones have still and video cameras and the capability to post those images or videos to the web, as well as the capability to browse the web.

- Keep all Internet access in a common location such as kitchens, dens, or living rooms, rather than behind the closed doors of bedrooms.

- Insist that children and teens show kindness and respect to others online just as they do in person. Tell them to talk to you if someone is mean or a bully.

- Don't allow any downloading or uploading of photos or videos without your permission.

- Insist that your children ask for your permission before signing up for any online accounts.

It is never too late to parent your children. You may find out that they are involved online in ways that surprise you, but you can set guidelines and establish a pattern of communicating going forward that helps to monitor and shape their behavior online.

CHAPTER 3

Online Bullying

Children and teens often face online cruelty (as well as cruelty in the real world). For younger kids, instant messaging and texting can become platforms for teasing and meanness. Teens often turn to social networking sites and blogs to detail conflicts or just to lash out.

Kids who bully online typically don't fit the stereotype of a playground bully. Children who have been identified as cyberbullies often have good, positive relationships with adults; they often perform well academically and have fine reputations. More often than not, they're some of the "good kids," and parents and teachers are left wondering why a good kid would behave in a cruel and hurtful way online.

Children and teens often use mean and harassing language online simply because they can. The anonymity that people feel behind a computer screen and the typical inability to see someone's face and hear their voice produces a phenomenon that psychologists call disinhibition. From the relative safety and isolation of a screen, lonely or bored children can strike out at others with little concern for the consequences. Without the social cues of face-to-face contact, it can be hard for children to really understand that they have hurt another person. The reduced social inhibition that comes with communicating through a screen empowers some kids to say or do things they would never say or do in person.

How to Keep Your Child from Being a Bully Online

Talk with your child about responsible behavior online. Undoubtedly you've already had many conversations with your child about how she should act in public places or with other people present, but she may not understand that she should apply that same wisdom to the online world. Talk to her about kindness, respect, and treating others as she would want to be treated herself—in the "real world" as well as online.

Be sure that your child understands that words that are read can hurt as deeply as words that are heard. Before she types something into a keyboard, she should ask herself if she would say the same thing if she were in the same room and looking the recipient in the eye.

Remind your child that anything she puts into any sort of electronic message can be forwarded (accidentally or on purpose) to anyone or everyone. Remind her that people other than the intended recipient may see the electronic message. Remind her that these messages can resurface and continue to hurt feelings and reflect badly on the sender, long after an angry or careless moment has passed.

Discourage your child from going online as part of a group. Often bullying happens during sleepovers, when kids feed off each other and may do things they wouldn't do while alone. Children and teens have an amazing capacity to talk each other into doing things that they later regret.

Do not allow children younger than 11 years old to have private email accounts, texting, or access to instant messaging. Young children are not developmentally ready for the language issues and split-second social decisions that typically arise with instant forms of text communication.

Look at the games your child plays on Xbox, PlayStation, or a web browser. Many games today can be played online with strangers from around the world, and they include the ability to chat with those strangers. If you permit your child to chat on gaming sites, you have a responsibility to make sure that he treats others with respect. These are competitive environments where the participants often use screen names that don't reveal their real-world identities, making the risk of disinhibition and rude behavior particularly high. (Note: You might not know that the average age of video gamers is 34. Consider carefully whether gaming sites are appropriate environments for your child or teen.)

How to Keep Your Child from Being Bullied Online

Bullying has been a part of many people's youth since long before the Internet was developed. In fact, many instances of online bullying are outgrowths of real-world bullying. So far, nobody has found a way to stop bullying altogether, but here are some simple, common-sense steps that you and your child can take to reduce the chance that she will be the target of an online bully.

You cannot look over your child's shoulder all the time, especially as she gets older, but it is vital that you be watchful for possible bullying that targets your child. Talk frequently with your child about her online activities. Stopbullying.gov, a government website managed by the U.S. Department of Health and Human Services, recommends that you set up a daily time to check in with your child. During your daily talks, you should be alert to any concerns your child might have about the things happening in her online world. Cover online harassing and bullying behaviors specifically, and encourage your child to tell you immediately if she sees someone being bullied or if she experiences bullying herself.

Recent studies have found that as few as 20% of cyberbullying victims ever tell adults about their experiences online. Given the number of kids who have experienced disrespect, meanness, or bullying, this statistic is disconcerting. When talking with your child about online bullying, keep in mind that the number-one thing that prevents most children from being honest with their parents is the fear that their parents will "pull the plug" on the technology. By having frequent conversations with your child about her online activity, you can begin to chip away at that reluctance to tell you about her online world. Reassure her that you want to help, not punish, if she experiences bullying or meanness online.

Know what websites and technologies your child uses when she goes online. Be familiar with those activities, and develop and enforce reasonable rules for your child's online time. As we discussed in Chapter 2, "Important Conversations," lay out your expectations for their online behavior, explain the rules you've established to ensure those expectations are met, describe how you will monitor their compliance with the rules, and be clear and specific about what will happen if the rules are broken.

It is important for you to have the passwords for your child's online accounts. Having routine access to online accounts *and checking them regularly* can help prevent a prolonged harassing conversation or event. We recommend having the passwords for all accounts of children under the age of 16. (Understand that having a password to a child's Facebook account is not the same as being "friended" by them. Just being a "friend" can greatly limit what you may be allowed to see.)

Your child should *think twice before posting or saying anything online.* That is one of those pieces of advice that is much easier to offer than it is to put into practice, especially for children and teens. But controlling impulses is a valuable skill to develop, online or off, and impulsive behavior online can have widespread and lasting consequences. Your child should be especially careful not to share secrets, gossip, post photos, or do anything else that could be used to embarrass her in a different context. Remind her that she has no control over how that information is used once it is in somebody else's hands. An awkward photo shared privately with a best friend one day can be posted widely the next day if the friend becomes angry or careless. Remind your child that her online language also helps establish her reputation.

Your child should check (again) all of the privacy settings and friends lists on her accounts, to be certain that she is sharing information only with people she knows and trusts. Even so, it won't hurt to remind her that once she shares information, she will have no control over how it is used in the future. It's a good idea for her to check privacy settings once a month and to pay attention to changes made to the privacy policies of any websites or services that she uses.

Signs of Bullying

The following signs can be evidence of bullying at school or online (they can also be indications of a variety of issues, ranging from normal adolescence to depression or other mental health troubles). If you see any of these signs in your child, get to the root of the problem. Your child may need your help and guidance, or may need help from professionals or school officials.

Is Your Child Being Bullied?

- Clothing or other belongings (electronics, jewelry, books, etc.) are missing or damaged

- Comes home with unexplained (or badly explained) injuries

- Seems to have not eaten lunch at school

- Seems angry, nervous, irritable, or depressed (especially right after school or being online)

Continued

- Appears to be afraid to go to school or wants to avoid specific places or activities

- Has recurrent bad dreams or other difficulty sleeping

- Frequently complains about headaches or stomachaches

- Loses interest in friends or has fewer friends

- Exhibits unexplained changes in eating habits

- Loses interest in school or scholastic performance drops

- Appears to feel helpless or unworthy

- Blames himself for problems outside of his control

- Cuts or otherwise hurts herself

- Talks about suicide

Is Your Child Bullying Others?

- Sometimes behaves violently

- Is repeatedly disciplined at school

- Has new possessions or money that she can't explain

- Frequently gets into verbal fights

- Needs to win or be the best at everything he does

- Won't take responsibility for her actions

- Is quick to blame others when issues develop

- Has friends or other family members who are bullies

What Should Your Child Do If Bullied?

If your child is being bullied or knows of someone being bullied online, he has the power to stop it. Share with your child the following list of things that he or she can do:

- **Do not respond to cyberbullying, and do not pass along or respond to any message or post that might be hurtful or embarrassing to you or others.** Many people who call names or who text or post offensive messages are simply hoping for a reaction—this is called *trolling*. Don't feed the trolls. Don't provide the reaction that they so desperately want. (This is *the* most important thing to say to your child!)

- **Tell your mom or dad or another adult you trust what is going on.** Nearly every adult has experience dealing with bullies. Talk with them about what you are going through and work with them to find ways to approach the problem.

- **Keep evidence of the bullying.** Make a log with the times, dates, and descriptions of every instance of cyberbullying. Save and print emails, text messages, and screenshots to support your log. Many states have enacted laws that specifically address cyberstalking and cyberharrassment. Cyberbully.us provides a brief review of state cyberbullying laws across the United States: www.cyberbullying.us/Bullying_and_Cyberbullying_Laws.pdf

- **Consider filing a complaint with the bully's service provider.** Often, everyone using a service has to agree to the terms of service, and those agreements often prohibit the harassment of other users.

- **If the bully is (or might be) from your school, report the cyberbullying to school authorities.** They can watch for face-to-face bullying that might follow your online encounter. The new laws in several states actually require school authorities to act on your behalf.

- **Block the bully.** Phone companies and many web services allow you to prevent specific people from contacting you through their systems.

- **Ask for help.** Sometimes bullying really hurts, and talking with a counselor can help you feel better. It can be an effective way to deal with the very real emotional pain that cyberbullying can produce.

What You Can Do If Your Child Is Being Bullied Online

We have seen the grave consequences of bullying on Facebook and other social networking sites played out in the news, including the suicides of teens who were subjected to extreme online and offline cruelty. What usually isn't talked about in the press are the less tragic, but still serious consequences of bullying online, such as loss of friendships, lowered self-esteem, feelings of shame, resentment, anger, and lower grades in school.

If you know or suspect that your child is being bullied, act quickly. Make the time to talk with your child. There is too much at stake to hope that the problem will go away by itself. Sympathize with your child and show that you understand and share her unease. Assure your child that she does not deserve to be treated this way and thank her for being brave in coming to you. Do not ask questions like, "Did you do something to annoy the bully?" That implies that your child provoked the bully and that the bully may have an excuse for his offensive behavior.

Tell your child not to respond in any way to a cyberbully. Responding directly to online bullying never solves the problem and, in fact, can make the situation worse. Bullies sometimes say hurtful things because the response they provoke makes them feel powerful. Warn your child to not take the bait.

Contact your child's school counselor or the school administration. Raise their awareness of the problem and see if they are able to help. Bullies are often known to their victims, and school authorities may be able to respond in ways to halt the bullying immediately. When adults get involved in incidences of bullying, the bullying tends to decrease or stop altogether. In whatever venue the online bullying has taken place (e.g., Facebook or a gaming community), insist that your child take a break from it to remove herself from the bullying.

Your primary job as a parent is to keep your child safe. If the bullying is criminal in nature or if you feel your child could be in danger, contact a law enforcement agency. Any of the following might be crimes:

- Threats of violence or implied violence

- Stalking or harassment

- Obscene phone calls or text messages

- Hate crimes (crimes based on the victim's membership in a social group, such as racial identity, religion, or gender)

- Photos or video taken in a place where the subject would expect privacy

- Sexual exploitation, child pornography, and sexting

- Extortion

- Impersonation

Be sure to follow up. Talk daily with your child to be certain that the bullying has ended. If it continues, you may need to start over again and try different approaches. At some point, you may even need to speak with an attorney to explore your options within the legal system.

CHAPTER 4

Kids, Privacy, and Technology

Privacy is one of those intangible rights that is easily eroded. Adults generally value privacy more than children or teens do. Adults also understand that losing one's privacy online can result in serious consequences, both financial and personal.

Online privacy is simply not on the radar of younger children using the Internet. And while teens might be concerned about their online privacy somewhat more than younger children, they too are naive and can be unaware, misled, or simply careless about their online activities when it comes to protecting their privacy. Inattention to privacy concerns can be especially risky now that we live in an age when many of the devices in our pockets and purses can broadcast things that were once easily kept private, including our exact location at any given moment, our bank account information, and our social security numbers.

How can you raise your children's awareness of both the need to keep some information private and the need to exercise special cautions online? Our recommendation is to create a multistep approach that is appropriate to the developmental level of your child.

All children, including teens, first need to understand what counts as personal information. Besides the obvious data such as name, address, home phone number, cell phone number, and birthday, point out that personal information includes such information as:

- Gender and age

- Name of school

- Teams, clubs, groups, and activities

- Personally identifying features such as a sports team jersey number, a performance schedule, screen names, or religious affiliation

- Friends lists on social media sites such as Facebook and Google+

- Photos uploaded to Facebook (especially if photos are tagged with names; also, most digital cameras tag photos with geolocation coordinates)

- Information about siblings, parents, or relatives

- Dates/times of family outings and vacations ("we're all going to a movie tonight!" tells the world that your home will be empty)

Elementary School–Age Children

Teach younger children (ages 5 through 11) what type of information is considered personal and that *it is never okay* to provide that information to anyone on the Internet without a parent's permission.

Younger children spend a great deal of their online time on gaming websites. Gaming websites will typically ask children to set up accounts, and setting up an account usually requires personal information. The personal information that game sites ask for can include your child's real name, age, email, and sometimes even a phone number and home address. Also, scammers and unscrupulous marketers target children who are using game sites, trying to extract even more information from them. Fraudulent ads on some game sites ask children for such information as their birth date, cell phone number, or even their mother's maiden name.

Children may receive scam emails disguised as emails from game site administrators, YouTube, iTunes, or even the FBI. These phony emails typically ask for login information, such as passwords, or for other personal information, such as social security numbers and more (this is called *phishing*). Sometimes these emails appear to be very official (that's the idea, after all), so the best strategy is for your young child to never give personal information without your permission, no matter who seems to be asking for it.

The difficulty for young children is that many websites legitimately require them to provide some personal information in order to use the site. If you want your child to be able to use a website that requires personal information, you will need to decide how comfortable you feel about providing your child's information, or whether you would rather use your own information and register your child under your name.

Middle School–Age Children

The risks for children in Grades 6 through 8 (ages 11 through 14) increase as they begin to explore more areas of the Internet and use applications that can reveal more personal information. Of course, it is still important that tweens and young teens understand what counts as personal information, and that they should be very careful what they reveal and to whom. However, they are also old enough to understand that information has value and that their personal information may be sold to marketers (legitimate and unscrupulous), spammers, or thieves. They should also understand that their online activities may be closely monitored by site hosts and marketers.

This age group should also be taught that *nothing is private online*. Though it may not be immediate or in every instance, sooner or later something your child has written or posted will be seen by someone whom it wasn't intended for. Ask your child: What if you sent a mean message about Kelly to Anna, and then Anna got mad at you and forwarded your message to Kelly? Your child may think this could never happen—but emphasize that it happens all the time.

Lack of Privacy

Merriam-Webster defines *privacy* as the state of being free from unauthorized intrusion. If your private information is seen by someone you didn't authorize to see it, it is no longer private. That is why we often say that there is no such thing as privacy on the Internet. It is practically impossible to restrict the viewing of material posted on the Internet to only the people it was intended for.

Explain that there are software "bots" and marketing tools that constantly "mine" personal data on the web. Data that your children intended to stay personal can be made public through deliberate hacking and also through more casual mistakes:

- Over-the-shoulder viewing, such as when a schoolmate (or his parent) looks at the display of your child's account

- A friend passes private texts or pictures to other friends

- Passwords to accounts are guessed, shared, or otherwise become known

- Lax account settings for a social network may expose private content to strangers (for example, friends of friends) or permit apps, games, or websites to access your child's accounts

- Account settings are changed by social networks and open users to more public settings (this has happened often to Facebook users)

- Phishing schemes may trick your child into revealing her website login credentials

- Scammers trick children into installing spyware onto their (or your) computer

- Users sometimes mistakenly post messages in public web areas that they assumed were private

- Parents may see postings of their children's friends while logged into their child's account (checking up on the child as part of agreed-upon rules)

High School–Age Teens

The risks for high school–age teens (ages 14 through 18) can be significant because some are exploring very risky behaviors, and much more can be at stake, including college acceptances, internships, and job opportunities. Also, when they sign up for activities such as team sports they often pledge to honor team behavior expectations. They often don't realize that some coaches and school administrators have the means and skills to monitor some online activities. Even when school personnel don't monitor online activities themselves, parents and other students may bring online proof of bad behavior to the attention of school officials. High school teens are also at risk because, as web-savvy as they consider themselves to be, they often trust their personal data with complete strangers—those friends of friends who proliferate on social networks.

In addition to the tips mentioned for the younger age groups, it's wise to do the following with your high school–aged child, both to reduce his risk of careless or inadvertent exposure online and to raise his awareness of the issues. First, ask your teen to read some recent articles about other kids who have experienced serious consequences as a result of their online behavior. It is tragically easy to find such articles by doing searches for the words *Facebook* and *teen* (or *kid*), combined with words like *arrested, suspended, fired,* or *disciplined.*

Next, because teens spend a great amount of time socializing on social networking sites, impress upon them that there is no privacy on such sites. Here are three examples of how private becomes public:

- In November 2011, Google became able to search and index AJAX and JavaScript content, meaning that Google was capable of searching any public page or forum, including public Wall postings on Facebook. This may have changed by the time of this publication; however, these kinds of "inadvertent" exposures happen routinely.

- Facebook's privacy settings typically change about three times a year, and sometimes those changes have reverted users' accounts back to more public settings. (In August 2012, the Federal Trade Commission finalized a settlement with Facebook that would prohibit Facebook from sharing information that was originally private without the explicit consent of the user. But the fact is, all of us will always be at the mercy of the people who run any website on which we share information.)

- Scammers routinely hack teens' Facebook accounts, both to gather information that has financial value and to trick teens into installing spyware that targets their parents. You and your teen should pay a visit to the excellent Facecrooks.com site for the latest information on scams making their way around Facebook.

According to our latest survey, the average high school junior has 802 Facebook friends. If your child has a similar number of friends, and he has set his account to permit "friend of a friend" viewing of content, and assuming each of his friends has 400 other unique friends, it would mean that your child is sharing personal information with more than *320,800 other people.* And according to a study conducted by TRUSTe, a leading online privacy solutions provider, 68% of teens "friend" complete strangers.

Social Media as a Burglary Tool

People who post photos to Facebook while they're on vacation or who use Twitter to announce how their meal is going in a restaurant may also be telling would-be criminals that their home is currently unoccupied.

UK home security experts Friedland recently surveyed 50 former burglars. Nearly 80% of the ex-burglars believe that modern burglars use social media to help select their targets. According to the ex-burglars, posting away-from-home activities on social media is among the top five most common home-security mistakes that homeowners make. (www.friedland.co.uk/en-GB/News/Pages/Whats-your-status.aspx)

Let your child know that when she installs Facebook add-ons (apps), she may be giving away the keys to her privacy completely. Many add-ons don't play by the rules, and abuse users' personal information. Some are nothing more than disguised malware. Ask your child to guess how many Facebook add-ons she thinks she has installed on her Facebook account—then ask her to log into Facebook and actually check. We recently did this with one teen and she was shocked to find 45 apps were using her personal data when she thought she had installed fewer than a dozen. It's easy to check which apps are permitted to interact with a Facebook account. Currently, you simply log in to Facebook, select Account Settings, and then select Apps from the left menu bar.

Teach your teen not to save passwords or personal information in web browsers. Encourage him to have different passwords for different website accounts. He should *never* use the same password for a bank account that he uses for any of his other accounts. Passwords should be at least eight characters and include a mix of uppercase and lowercase letters, plus numbers and symbols such as = @ %.

Impress upon your teen that we all leave digital footprints everywhere we go online or when using smartphones. These digital footprints can be impossible to erase and can become part of your child's online reputation. Everyone from employers to internship directors and college admissions officers is using the Internet to evaluate candidates' online reputations, and their probing includes examining social networking sites such as Facebook. If your teen has any doubts about this, ask her to enter the following search terms into a search engine and review some of the articles that appear: *college admissions, Facebook,* and *reject.*

CHAPTER 5

Online Gaming

One of the primary reasons that kids flock to the Internet, especially children under 14, is to play games. The two most popular current game sites that kids talk about wherever we go are Miniclip (www.miniclip.com) and AddictingGames (www.addictinggames.com). However, kids visit a wide range of game sites such as Rebubbled, Armor Games, Max Games, Y8, ActionFlash, and XGen Studios. AddictingGames is owned by Viacom, the firm that owns the Nickelodeon Network, home of popular cartoons such as *SpongeBob SquarePants* and *The Penguins of Madagascar*. All of these popular game sites are designed to appeal to tween-age children, ages 10 to 13, but children as young as 6 and 7 visit them regularly.

Although many games on these sites are harmless entertainment, some of the games are plainly intended for mature audiences and are completely inappropriate for younger children because of the games' sexual, violent, or vulgar content. And many of these games are an easy click away from adult content. For example, a popular game that has appeared on several of these game sites is "Whack Your Boss." A link is provided from the game to the company's website, where the visitor will find scatological and grotesquely violent animations, as well as ads for online casinos and sex surveys.

Cartoon violence has been around for as long as there have been cartoons. However, the level of animated violence displayed by online games covers a wide range and, at the far end of the spectrum, can be extreme and gory. Some of these violent games depict violence against women, sometimes with sexual overtones. Nudity, sex, and drug references also find their way into some animated game offerings. The rules you set for your child should make very clear your stance on games of this nature.

How Safe Are Dress-Up Games?

A very popular game and social site for young girls is Stardoll.com. Girls in fourth grade through seventh grade will often tell us that they have accounts on this site.

Though Stardoll, and other sites like it, make an effort to keep their content safe and appropriate, we have found offensive screen names and posts on Stardoll every time we've visited. The offensive content usually takes the form of very sexual or vulgar postings. Fortunately, they are rare, but parents need to be aware that sites like these are not able to police their entire community with human eyes. Instead, typically software is employed to look for offending words. It is easy, however, for users to hide or mask their offensive selections by substituting characters, such as the number 5 for the letter S, and thus go unnoticed by the software.

Bottom line: Though the risks are small, there are no guarantees for parents that your children won't come in contact with sexually offensive material or the people who create it on Stardoll.com.

Game Sites Aren't Nannies

There are tens of thousands of games available on children's game sites, and some of the sites even give users the option of creating their own games and uploading them for others to play. With such large volumes, it would be difficult for gaming-site managers to police their site content perfectly. Furthermore, the revenue for these sites comes largely from advertisers who pay according to the number of site visitors, setting up an obvious conflict of interest. Lurid content may be inappropriate for children, but it attracts visitors (and therefore advertising dollars).

Even if game-site managers are diligent about excluding the bad games and about labeling their remaining content appropriately, you have to rely on your child to follow the site's guidelines. But if an unsupervised fifth grade boy is presented with a set of games with ratings ranging from "E" for Everyone to "M" for Mature, that fifth grader's natural curiosity is likely to lead him to select the "M" game.

The message here is simple. Don't assume that all of the content on a children's game site is suitable for children. Don't assume that all the content is consistent with your family values or is free of stereotypes and media messages. Finally, don't assume that your child will scrupulously follow a game site's guidelines for selecting age-appropriate entertainment.

What to Do

The AddictingGames website offers good advice on its "For Parents" page. They urge parents to "identify which games are appropriate for their particular household" by considering your child's "unique personality and level of maturity." They advise that you watch your child play and talk with him about the games he plays (and also suggest that you try playing the games yourself). Finally, they suggest that if you are not able to supervise your child's play and aren't comfortable with what he might do on his own, you should consider installing parental control software that blocks AddictingGames and other game sites.

Take an active role in your child's online world. Look at the game sites your child wants to play on, look at the games they want to play, watch them play, and talk with them about their games. If you cannot be there all the time (and who can?), look at your options for parental control software that we've listed in the Tools and Resources section, or listed on our website at ChildrenOnline.org. Then visit your local software store, or shop online, and purchase gaming software that you find educational or appropriate for entertainment. Good online sites to purchase game software include:

- Software for Kids: www.softwareforkids.com

- Children's Software Online: www.childrenssoftwareonline.com

- All Educational Software: www.alleducationalsoftware.com

- Funbrain: www.funbrain.com

- Poptropica: www.poptropica.com (Warning: players are allowed to chat)

- PBS Kids: www.pbskids.org

Concerns about Minecraft

Have you heard about Minecraft? It is very likely that your children have, even though the game only came out in late 2011. The game has skyrocketed in popularity with children from ages 7 to young teens.

Minecraft is a creative, open-ended video game in which participants build things out of textured cubes in a 3-D-like world. There are several versions and modes of game play (including survival, creative, and adventure) all of which make use of creative problem solving skills.

Minecraft does not contain the kind of violence as seen in Call of Duty Black Ops, Halo 3 or even Batman Arkham City Lockdown (all rated as not suitable for kids under 15 by Common Sense Media). Minecraft, by contrast, is a breath of fresh air

Continued

among the graphically violent video game genre. There are still concerns about the game, however.

The concerns we have heard about from parents and in online blogs can be summed up as follows:

- There is an addictive nature to the game and parents are concerned about the hours and hours that their children spend playing it. This screen time is sometimes at the expense of time spent doing things like talking face-to-face with friends, bike-riding, playing outside games, and doing homework.

- The game is typically played via private, non-moderated Minecraft servers. Thus, playing Minecraft offers an opportunity for children to interact with strangers, some of whom may be older teenagers.

- The multiplayer version of the game offers the ability to chat with other players and parents have voiced concerns about profanity-laced conversations.

- Like most online interactive communities without parental supervision, cyberbullying has been reported. This game is especially prone to "griefing," which occurs when a user's goal is to annoy or anger other players rather than to play the game, sometimes through the destruction of the other players' structures.

The growing tension parents feel around this creative, fun video game highlights the fact that parents need to set limits and boundaries for their children's use of the Internet. Parents can limit time spent online and who their children play Minecraft with. They can set conditions, such as allowing game play only after adequate time is given to homework and chores, and make sure that playtime contains a healthy mix of time spent outside, with friends in "real life," on a bike, involved with sports, and other activities. However, we would add that children as young as 7 to 9 years old should avoid playing multiplayer video games. We also do not recommend chatting or socializing online before age 12. If your younger children want to play Minecraft, you can still allow them to play, but with limited chat and limited screen time.

One last reminder: as we mentioned earlier, the average age of online gamers at some of the most popular video games is 34. Most of these games have a chat feature. Think carefully about your child's maturity before allowing her to participate.

CHAPTER 6

Social Networks

Currently the most popular social networking site for teens is Facebook. The great majority of students in eighth grade and beyond have Facebook accounts, and children as young as eight years old are creating accounts.

As wonderful as Facebook is for adults and older teens who wish to connect with friends and family, it is first and foremost a business designed to make money. The decisions made by Facebook sometimes put profits ahead of our children's privacy, safety, or best interests. For example, just a few years ago, Facebook recommended that users be at least 16 years old to use it. Today, 13 years old is the minimum age to use Facebook. The recommended age did not decrease to 13 because Facebook research determined that the site is developmentally healthy and appropriate for 13-year-olds. Facebook reduced its minimum user age to 13 to increase its user base (and thus revenue).

Other Social Networks Increasing in Popularity

Twitter is beginning to get kids' attention and a growing percent are signing up for accounts enabling them to "tweet" about their life to their friends. Instagram, a photo-sharing app with a social networking component, is growing in popularity among younger children in sixth through eighth grade. Google+ is becoming popular for children in fifth through seventh grade. Though many children are told by their parents that they cannot have a Facebook account at these younger ages, the children are easily finding substitutes.

The age of 13 was almost certainly chosen because that is the minimum age designated by the Federal Trade Commission's Children's Online Privacy Protection Act. COPPA rules greatly restrict the online advertising that can be aimed at children under 13, as well as limiting what a website can do with user information. As a result of COPPA, many websites won't accept users who admit that they're under the age of 13. However, it's very easy for children 12 and younger to lie about their age and get an account on websites with age limits.

As of the end of 2012, Facebook has claimed to have one billion users. Facebook has grown so tremendously large that it is impossible for the site managers to successfully police users, all uses of the site, and all third-party applications. In 2011, *Consumer Reports* magazine reported that there were about 7.5 million children in the United States under the age of 13 using Facebook. Scams are rampant and very successfully directed at naive and unsuspecting teens. (Visit Facecrooks.com for a review of up-to-date scams targeting Facebook users.) Fortunately, there are things you can do to make Facebook a safer experience for your teen. We have some tips and suggestions for topics to discuss with your teen regarding her Facebook account. As you may have guessed, you will need to play an active role in her use of this very popular online hangout.

Am I the Customer or the Product?

If you are a Facebook user, you might wonder how it has become such a valuable company. It seems puzzling. After all, Facebook doesn't directly sell you anything. You pay nothing to socialize with your friends on Facebook.

A wise participant in an online community (blue_beetle on MetaFilter) explained the solution to this puzzle nicely: "If you are not paying for it, you're not the customer; you're the product being sold."

The value of Facebook lies in its users, who, as they travel the web, provide Facebook's massive database with rich insights into their interests and behaviors. That database is used to do very sophisticated targeting of advertisements, a service that Facebook provides to advertisers at a price advertisers are happy to pay. Facebook earns 85% of its revenue from advertising.

What is a Friend?

It has become common to hear the phrase, "He friended me." That awkward term refers to the online idea of friend, as in, "He contacted me to be his friend online." Just what exactly is a friend online? A friend online can mean many things. An online friend might indeed be a real-life friend your child already knows and hangs out with. An online friend can be someone you once knew in person years ago and are now back in contact with. An online friend can be a friend of a friend, or simply an acquaintance or business contact who wants to know you better. And, in the case of thousands of teens, an online friend can be someone they have never met or had any connection to whatsoever, except for the "friend request" they received one day.

With the popularity of social networking sites, children and teens are finding themselves making complicated decisions about online friends every day. Should they confirm that someone is a friend? How do they know that this someone will be thoughtful and kind? Should they trust this person with their personal information? Could this prospective friend really be an advertising "bot" (computer program) designed to use or misuse their information to sell them things? The broader question is, are children and young teens ready to be making these decisions every day? Do they really understand the risks?

Managing an Online Friend Collection

If your teen is actively engaged in texting, social networking, and instant messaging, it would not be unusual for him to have as many as a thousand online friends. These friends may have access to his social network personal pages, containing pictures, information, and insights about the sort of person your child is. Your child may claim otherwise, but it's highly unlikely that he has a thousand friends. His online friend collection likely contains many, many people he knows little or nothing about.

With that in mind, here are some ways you can help your child manage his online friend collection:

- Begin having conversations early with your child about online friendship. With the popularity of Webkinz and Club Penguin, young children are facing the task of understanding whom to trust online.

- Have frequent conversations with your child. Discuss her online reputation. Nothing can substitute for your wisdom and values in helping your kids deal with friendships, either in person or online.

- Allow your children to only have online friends whom they both know in person and *trust*. You can take it one step further and allow your children to only have friends online whom you know in person and trust.

- Sit down with your child and go through your child's buddy or friend list on instant messaging, iChat, Skype, Instagram, and gaming and social networking sites. If you don't know a person on the friend list and your child isn't sure how he knows that person, remove that name from the list.

- Look with your teen at her Facebook Wall and Photo pages. Make sure her pages are free of cruel language, provocative or incriminating pictures, or information that she wouldn't want to become public. Do the same for any other social networking sites she belongs to.

- Remind your child that nothing is private online, and once something is posted, she no longer has any control over how that post might be used by others.

- Talk to your child about the impersonal nature (and sometimes anonymity) of online interactions, and about how much easier it is for people interacting remotely to misunderstand one another, or even to be cruel or harassing.

- Set time limits for your child's screen time.

- Encourage your child to have real-world encounters with friends, and do what you can to make real-world get-togethers happen on a regular basis.

- Create rules for online relationships. For example, do not allow a teen to have a long term (two weeks in Internet time) chatting relationship without at least one conversation in real life.

- Consider contacting the parents of the friends in your child or young teen's buddy or friend list. Explain to your child that it's the same as getting to know the parents of his real-world friends, which happens naturally at places like school meetings and events, youth sporting events, and so on. If you can establish a relationship with parents of his online friends, you can create group rules around their time spent online, something that will be good for everyone.

It is difficult to navigate the world of friendship, especially for young teens today who spend much of their time texting, Facebook chatting, or instant messaging. A critical component of child development is the process of learning trust, friendship, and intimacy, but it is a process that can be fraught with disappointment and dishonesty. For generations, kids have struggled to understand the subtleties of true friendships on playgrounds and in back-yards, and now, on the Internet. As parents, we can use the wisdom we've acquired during our own learning processes to help guide our children through these sometimes painful challenges. We can apply some of the things we've learned about life in the real world to our children's online world.

A Look at Terms of Service

Sit down with your child and explore together the terms of service and privacy policy on Facebook. Have a discussion about what the two policies mean, and what some possible implications might be. Now find similar information on YouTube, Instagram, and other social networks.

Ask your child how the policies might affect her. Help her to be a critical consumer.

Facebook evolves constantly, so we're not going to give you step-by-step advice on account settings. Instead, we'll provide some examples of what to consider when looking at the terms of service on Facebook, or on any site. As always, safety and privacy remain top of mind.

Below are examples of some features and policies on Facebook that have been in effect in the past. Some may still be in effect. Discuss each of these with your child. Most of the items in this list can be turned on and off, depending on the settings your child has chosen for her account:

- Facebook can sell your posted photos and videos without your permission and without compensating you.

- Facebook can use your profile photo in Facebook ads to your friends.

- Facebook apps can take your personal info and sell or use it without your permission.

- Friends can sign you up for groups without your permission.

- Complete strangers can review your list of friends.

- Search engines can be used to search some of your profile information or list of friends.

- Everything you ever posted on your Facebook Wall since you opened your account was reposted when Facebook launched Timeline in early 2012.

- Facebook shares your profile information with advertisers to determine what products and services you purchase on other websites. Facebook then uses this information in advertising to your friends.

Help your child think of possible implications of some of these items.

On many websites, terms of service and privacy policies change on a regular basis. In some cases, when the policies change, all users' account settings revert to default settings. Your child should review her account settings on all social networks on a regular basis. Emphasize to her that she has control over how her personal information is used—*but she must choose to exert that control.*

Photo Tagging

Under the default settings, when people post photos on Facebook, they have the option of attaching the names of people who appear in the photos, a process called *tagging*. Unfortunately, anyone or anything can be tagged as your child. Incorrect tagging may be innocent (a common joke is to tag each of the kittens in a basket, or some other collection of objects, with the names of friends), but it can also be more sinister. A photograph of someone doing something embarrassing or illegal, especially if his or her face is not clearly visible, can accidentally or deliberately be tagged as your child and then automatically join the other photos in her profile.

As of this writing, there is no easy way to prevent mischievous or malicious photo tagging on Facebook (or anywhere else). Your child should be vigilant whenever she receives a notice that she has been tagged in a photo and should view the photo immediately to make sure it is appropriate. Additionally, photo tagging is yet another reason why you must emphasize with your child that she should avoid having photos of herself taken that could come back to haunt her. Examples include photos where alcohol use is obvious or implied and photos of the child in provocative poses. It's an unfortunate aspect of the online world.

Recommendations for Posting Pictures

- Talk to your children and set guidelines about the content of photos or videos they are allowed to post and where they are allowed to post them.

- Remind your child that once another person gets hold of any picture, that photo can be copied, altered, reposted publicly, or sent directly to anyone else.

- Do not allow your child or teen to send pictures over their cell phones without your permission.

- Do not allow your child or young teen to post any picture or video online without your permission. Very young children should not be allowed to post any pictures or videos of themselves or others, period.

- Ask to see your teen's social networking sites (including Instagram and YouTube) and check them for inappropriate pictures or videos.

- When using Facebook, Google+, or MySpace, your teen should keep their friend list limited to people they know personally and set the viewing restrictions to "Friends Only."

- Make sure that all online accounts with photo or video content are set to restrictive privacy settings that do not allow strangers to view the content.

- When using commercial sites geared for storing photos, do some research first and find out what controls you have for protecting your family pictures.

- Teach your child to speak up to their friends when they don't want their picture taken, posted, or tagged.

It's Not All Bad!

Social networks such as Facebook and YouTube are useful and enjoyable tools that have revolutionized the way people connect with one another. Using these websites can be great fun, but their proper use requires a great deal of thought and careful decision-making.

CHAPTER 7

Cell Phones
and Smartphones

Years ago, when the first cellular telephones appeared, they were big and clunky (but still incredibly cool) and all you were able to do with them was make phone calls. Because they were cumbersome and expensive, and not many people had one, not everyone saw the need to own one. Today, nearly everyone carries a cell phone that weighs just ounces and can function as a media player, alarm clock, address book, calculator, calendar, gaming device, camera, and mobile Internet browser, as well as a telephone. Thousands of downloadable apps allow smartphones to do almost anything, it seems!

Parents everywhere are wrestling with the question of when to give a cell phone to their children. According to our research, 25% of fourth graders say they have a cell phone, 73% have a cell phone in sixth grade, and by the time kids are in eighth grade, 93% have a cell phone, and nearly all of these eighth graders have texting ability.

Ask adults the reasons they provided their child with a phone, and *safety* is the most frequent answer. Ask a child or teen why they need a phone, and *connecting to friends, texting, playing games, accessing social networks, viewing media,* and *taking pictures* will be the frequent answers.

Be a Shining Example

It's probably easy for you to come up with rules for your child's phone use. "Don't use your phone at the dinner table." "Don't interrupt a face-to-face conversation to take a phone call." "Don't use your phone while driving." "Turn off your phone during family time."

It's harder to obey those same rules yourself, but *you* are the example your child is most likely to learn from. So it is important that you serve as a good role model for your child. Actions speak far louder than words.

Use and Misuse of Cell Phones

With safety quite rightly on the minds of parents, cell phones seem to be a good idea in today's increasingly challenging world. Parents find the idea of immediate connection with their child very comforting. Yet a state-of-the-art smartphone is much more than a safe connection to a parent. It is a powerful mini-computer with the ability to perform many functions, including texting, gaming, surfing the web, or taking pictures or videos—and then sending them to the web or to other phones. In the hands of children, many of those functions can be risky and when used inappropriately they can actually jeopardize children's safety.

Results from our 2010–11 research survey of more than 2,000 students illustrates these risks:

- 10.7% of all student cell-phone owners say they have received "offensive or inappropriate photos or videos." The terms "offensive or inappropriate" were not defined—children were left to evaluate those terms for themselves.

- 14.8% of students whose phones could receive texts reported receiving "offensive, harassing, or hurtful text messages."

- 49.7% of all students reported receiving ads on their cell phones. (Some companies target cell phone users with scam ads that result in charges to cell phone bills, a fraudulent practice called "cramming.")

The Pew Internet study series of 2010, a project of the Pew Research Center, describes similar risks:

- 26% of teens say they have been bullied or harassed through texting.

- 15% of teens admit to receiving text messages containing sexually suggestive nude or nearly nude images of someone they know (sexting).

- 64% of teens say they text during class.

- 30% of teens estimate that they text at least 100 times daily.

- 34% of driving-age teens admit to texting while driving.

Texting While Driving: Don't!

The biggest phone-related threat to your teen's physical wellbeing, by far, stems from texting while driving. It may come as a surprise, but for a driver, reading or writing text can have a bigger effect on reaction times than the effects that come from being drunk.

Car and Driver magazine conducted an experiment in 2009 that involved driving a Honda Pilot on an empty taxiway at an airport. The car was fitted with a red light on the windshield to simulate the brake lights of a leading car. The drivers, an editor and an intern at the magazine, were instructed to hit the brakes as soon as the red light went on, and a computer measured their reaction times.

They measured reaction times and stopping distances undistracted, and then compared that baseline to reaction times while reading and typing texts. Then the two test subjects split a fifth of vodka and tried again with their blood alcohol above 0.08% (legally drunk in all 50 states as of 2011).

Average reaction response times increased for all activities, but delays were greater from texting than from drinking. But, as the magazine pointed out, averages don't tell the whole story. For the slowest reaction while texting at 35 mph, the car traveled an extra 188 feet, and for the slowest 70 mph reaction, the car traveled an extra 319 feet—more than the length of a football field—before the driver hit the brakes. The full results are found online at the *Car and Driver* website (www.caranddriver.com/features/texting-while-driving-how-dangerous-is-it).

You've probably already talked with your teen about drinking and driving, and made him promise *never* to get into a car with a driver who's been drinking. You need to have a similar discussion about texting while driving. It's not enough for your teen to be a safe driver himself; your child needs to understand and feel strongly that he also cannot ever be a passenger in a car with a texting driver. His future may depend on it.

A Not-So-Smart Phone with Usage Controls Might Be the Answer

We all want to provide the best for our children, but sometimes the best isn't more, it's less. When it comes to a cell phone for your child, a simple cell phone might make more sense than a smartphone, especially if it's your child's first phone. A basic cell phone without a camera is the safest option, although such phones are getting more and more difficult to find. A recent check of AT&T's wireless phone offerings found only 3 of its 88 phones available without a camera.

You may not be able to find a suitable basic phone without a built-in camera, but your wireless provider can give you options to control how your child uses his phone. Of course, there's an extra monthly charge to have some of these extra controls, but you'll be saving money on the phone and data plan, compared to what you'd be paying for a smartphone. Plus, the additional measure of safety and privacy may be well worth any added expense.

Go to your wireless provider's website and type "parental controls" into the search box. Most providers let you restrict the times of day (or night) that your child can use his phone, as well as let you set total usage allowances for text or voice within a billing period. You can also usually block specific numbers from calling in or out from your child's phone, as well as setting safe numbers (for example, your cell or home number) that your child can call—even if he is out of usage time or it is during a time you have chosen to restrict usage.

When it's time for your teen to make the move to a smartphone, most providers offer content filters that can be adjusted to limit purchases, videos, games, music, apps, or the websites that your child can access with the smartphone. When possible, wait until your child is at least age 15 to get him a smartphone.

Ask your wireless carrier about all of your options. If you don't find a time-of-use restriction strategy that works for you, consider collecting all of your children's smartphones at night to keep them from texting and using the Internet during the night.

Another option is to consider the purchase of a Kajeet phone or smartphone (www.kajeet.com). Kajeet phones are specifically designed for parents who want to have greater control over their child's cell phone usage and access to features. The phones can even include content filtering.

CHAPTER 8

Teaching Your Child to Be Savvy

You have undoubtedly run across browser pop-ups, banner ads, and unsolicited emails that offer links to prizes, deep-discount offers, miracle cures, naughty pictures, celebrity gossip, and more. Most adults have enough savvy to know that these links lead to nothing worthwhile.

How do we protect our children from online scammers who use flashy advertising or misleading emails? One important approach is to think of ways that you yourself have been misled or tricked in the past, and share those examples with your child. If we can also help our children understand, on a more fundamental level, the psychological tricks that scammers use, our kids will be empowered to see through the old tricks and be ready to recognize and avoid the new scams as they're invented.

That said, younger children are not developmentally ready to understand the risks that scams represent, or to recognize the subtle psychological tricks that scammers use. Because of this, we do not recommend that children below sixth grade (age 11) have their own private email accounts or be permitted to browse the web without restriction.

Typical Scam Advertising Directed at Kids

Our online clicks, purchases, word searches, and browsing behaviors are monitored, tracked, and analyzed. Great effort is made to tempt us to click on banner ads and fill out surveys, and scam artists coax us into revealing personal information that can be sold, used for marketing purposes, or worse. And the "netizens"—citizens of the Internet—most vulnerable to these efforts are children. Children often do not understand the value of privacy and cannot understand the many consequences of lost privacy. These issues go well beyond even identity theft.

If a caring adult has not taught them otherwise, children will reveal almost anything online in exchange for a reward or gift. Popular kid's sites, including gaming sites and gaming cheat-code sites, often display ads that target tweens or young teens with come-ons such as "Are you a good kisser?," "Who will you marry?," and "Are you datable?" If your child takes one of these quizzes, they may be told that the testers will text the results to her cell phone number. The real outcome of your child's quiz-taking comes when you start seeing bogus subscriptions charged to her number on your phone bill.

Along with the quizzes are the ever-present "Free ringtones!" "Win the race!" and "Bonk the bunny!" banners. And then there are the plethora of scams and deceitful ads announcing that "You are the 999,999th visitor and a winner!" or that you'll "Receive a free" iPad, iPhone, laptop, cash award, or any number of other things nearly any child would want. All are intended to fool our kids into giving out private information.

Children today need to understand that this virtual adscape is designed to extract personal information from them, and that their personal information is just another form of money or worse to the scammers and marketers who target them.

What Makes Scams Work?

Scams usually involve a proposal or offer that appears to fulfill a need or want. For kids, that might be currency that's used in an online game they enjoy, a free iPad or game console, intimate pictures of a celebrity, music, ringtones, or free access to a pay-only website.

The second thing that makes scams work is the social engineering techniques used in the presentation of the proposal or offer. Social engineering is the art of manipulating people's behavior. For example, scammers may make their message personally interesting, or make it look like the message came from someone their victim trusts. Some of the social engineering techniques out there are quite sophisticated and fool adults as well as children.

Tricks Scammers Use

Here are some social engineering techniques that are commonly used by advertisers and scammers who try to exploit our children. Talk with your child about these concepts. The more aware your child is of how these feelings are exploited, the more likely it is that he will not be fooled.

Flattery/Insecurity. Kids, especially adolescents, are often insecure about some aspects of their lives or personal appearance. Sites that urge them to click on a link to find out if they're attractive in some way to their peers are almost always scams.

Curiosity. Some ads play on children's natural curiosity. Ads that urge a child to find out things like "the secret that game companies don't want you to know" or "what your teachers aren't telling you" are examples of this commonly used trick.

Authority. For kids online, this technique will usually take the form of emails claiming to be from a current service provider (anyone they have an online account with) or from some representative of the government (typically the police, the FBI, or the U.S. Department of Homeland Security). We spend a lot of time encouraging our children to cooperate with authority figures, so it is not surprising that scammers try to trick our kids by pretending to be authorities. The logos are real (because they are copied from real websites), but the scammers behind them are not. No reputable company will ask for a password in an email; the FBI will never ask questions by email.

Scarcity. "Hurry, there are only two left!" or "The offer expires in three minutes." This is a very effective ploy because it demands quick action with little thought. Nobody wants to miss something just because she hesitated.

Social Proof. When a company tries to convince people to use its product or service because "everybody" is using it, this is a warning sign. Children should be encouraged to do their research and make decisions based on their needs, not on what they think other people may (or may not!) have done.

Likability. It is natural for people to give more consideration to offers from people or companies that seem likable. Kids need to learn how to separate the offer from the person or company making the offer.

Teach your child that advertisers and scammers will use these tricks and others to try to manipulate him. Help him be a smart consumer who doesn't fall for these common techniques.

Social Engineering in Emails

Some of the folks who send spam emails are brilliant social engineers. One of their greatest talents is manipulating the behavior of the recipient. They must first get your attention with a subject line that will entice you to open the email. There have been thousands of effective subject lines like those that follow.

Continued

Ask yourself if you or your child would have opened email carrying any of these subject lines.

Order #42396	*There's a problem with your profile*
Join our club	*Your opinion could be worth $$*
Your request denied	*Error in processing*
Photos from the weekend	*Ann Parker sent you a message on Facebook*
Books you need	*Free downloadable preview*
Mistake in your file	*Someone replied to your comment*
Answers for exams	*Why don't you email me?*
Your comment erased	*Your email exceeded the storage limit*
You're just so stupid	*Your account is about to expire*

Once you have opened the email, the scammer must next trick you into doing one of two things, either clicking on a link or double-clicking an attached file. The link or file name will match the fake subject of the email (for example, the "Subject: Order #42396" email may simply contain a file named "invoice," or the "Subject: Photos from the weekend" email may contain a zipped file named "photos"). Any email may simply contain a variation of the line, "Click here if you have trouble reading this email," along with some broken image links.

Clickable links in these sorts of emails may take you to a drive-by download site, and any attached files are likely to include a Trojan horse that contains malware. The software that gets installed as a result may do anything, up to and including giving complete control of your personal computer to the scammers who sent you the email.

Younger children and teens are especially at risk. Younger children have little or no understanding of the disguised threats that pour into email accounts. Teens are exactly those who are most likely to click links disguised as notifications from Facebook, Twitter, YouTube, porn sites, or purporting to be funny or embarrassing celebrity videos. Have a discussion with your child about the tricks that scammers use, and about what can happen to a computer that becomes infected with malware.

Good Old-Fashioned Fraud

Variations of these fraud schemes were around long before the Internet, but have become much more widespread because of the ease of advertising on websites or of sending spam emails. Fortunately, most "traditional" fraud schemes require money to be spent, something that is not easy for most children to do online, since most do not have credit or debit cards. Even so, you should talk with your child about these scams, so that she is aware of them by the time she does have a credit card or PayPal account. And watch out if your child asks to "borrow" your credit card for a seemingly harmless or inexpensive-sounding offer!

"Free" goods. Ask yourself how a legitimate business can make a profit by giving away its products for free. Very often, there is a small shipping or handling charge that needs to be put onto a credit card. Later, you might find that those sources have used your credit card information to attach a worthless (to you) monthly subscription charge to your account. Free ringtones and phone games require a cell phone number to complete the transaction, and cell phone numbers are sometimes used to attach subscription charges to your phone bill. (This is called "cramming.")

Personal weight or pimple control. Weight loss, muscle gain, and pimple-control ads are sometimes targeted at young people. Adolescents, especially, are often very concerned about their physical appearance, but go to your family physician to ask about these sorts of products. Unregulated miracle cures sold over the web are useless at best, and at worst can be dangerous. Your doctor will know the state of the art and will have access to legitimate healthcare products and treatments. And teach your teen to beware of ads pushing more dangerous drugs that claim to build muscle quickly.

Deeply discounted software. Deeply discounted software is often a foreign version or an illegal copy, or it has adware or spyware embedded. Check the online reputation of any unfamiliar software vendors before you decide to give them your business.

Phishing

Phishing emails are designed to look as though they came from a legitimate (and often well-known) organization. For instance, your child might receive an email that appears to be from a site administrator for Facebook or from a gaming site, complete with the brand logos and graphic styling. Phishers will make these emails look very real. The email will usually say that there is a problem with your account or with a shipment that they are trying to send to you, or it might say that some other user on the service has complained about something you did. They use social engineering to get you to click on a link, supposedly in order to deal with a problem.

These emails are usually intended to trick you into going to a fake website to reveal private information. Often, the link shown in the email appears to be legitimate, but clicking on it takes you to a different, underlying link. The fake websites are skillfully designed to look official. You may be asked to provide a login name and password or to verify your identity by providing personal details about yourself.

In some cases, a phishing email will be easy for your child to spot. No sophisticated online business will ever ask one of its customers to send personal or account information by email. If your child receives an email asking for an email reply with such information, she will know that it is really from a scammer phishing for the data.

If your child receives an email from a site or service she uses that asks her to follow a link to resolve an issue, she should be taught to *never* click the link, but to ask you for assistance. If you think the email might be genuine, navigate to the site using your browser's address bar or by using an existing personal bookmark. If you cannot find or resolve the issue on the site, contact the site's customer service group and ask them about the email.

In any case, we must emphasize again that you and your child should never follow links that appear in unsolicited email, texts, wall posts, instant messages (IMs), or chats. The bogus links in scammers' emails, texts, wall posts, and IMs might not only lead to phishing sites, they can also lead to sites that try to install malware on your computer.

Rules for Ads and Links

The list of fraudulent, deceitful scamming ads on children's websites is endless. Many lead to spyware, adware, and inappropriate content. Just because a website is designed for children doesn't mean that it carries only safe or appropriate advertising. Children Online (ChildrenOnline.org) recommends that parents have a conversation with their children about the sites they use. Visit sites with your children and talk about the advertising that is aimed at them. Teach them:

- not everyone on kids' websites has their best interests in mind

- never give out *any* personal information

- clicking on website ads *can* cause harmful software to be installed on your computer

- if it seems too good to be true, it is

- advertising doesn't have to be truthful

- it is easy to deceive others online, including through advertising

- if they are ever unsure, scared, or upset by what happens to them online, they should come talk to you about it immediately

Unfortunately, a small number of unscrupulous people make everyone's Internet use risky. We must constantly be skeptical and on our guard, and that is what we should be teaching our children as they grow up using the Internet.

Software Protection

You can protect your child to some extent by using the spam filters available in most email programs. Also, many email providers have user-adjustable spam filters available as an account setting. No spam filter is perfect, though, and some spam will always make it through. Having a filter catches most of the junk, but it does not eliminate the need to educate your child.

Make sure you are using a firewall—software that protects computers and routers from some types of Internet connections. There are also a number of software solutions that detect and protect your computer from malware, but research them carefully before you install them. Fake antivirus software is a common Trojan horse used to introduce malware into computers. Make sure you get a quality anti-spyware program from a legitimate source. Those who own Apple computers are also at risk and need to have quality anti-spyware software installed. (Once upon a time, there were very few attacks on Apple computers. That is no longer the case, however.)

Once you have installed and configured your software, keep it up to date and do not let your subscription to updates expire. If your computer is connected to the Internet, most modern software will check periodically for updates and will advise you when updates are available. Software updates are often specifically related to security flaws that have been discovered in your version of the software, so quickly fixing those defects will leave you and your child more secure. As you might expect, it is especially important to keep your web browser and anti-spyware software up to date.

Finally, do not be lulled into a false sense of security by the software safe-guards that you install. Scammers know that the easiest way into a computer is almost always through mistakes made by the user. Their skill with social engineering and the ability to distribute their scams to tens of thousands of potential victims at a time ensures the occasional success. And as long as they occasionally succeed, they will keep improving their scams and keep trying to find new victims.

It's Not About Technology, It's About Taking Care of Our Children

The one constant we can count on is that just when we figure out an electronic gadget or Internet site, a new one will pop up on the scene. It is almost impossible to keep up with the speed of technology. The good news is that understanding technology and its rapid changes is less important than understanding your child. Often the best answers to protecting and monitoring your child online have nothing to do with technology. They involve making the same common-sense decisions for limits and rules that you have been making for your kids since they first grabbed for a hot or sharp object.

Just as we set up boundaries and limits for our children, they push back, wanting more and more independence. This tension has been a critical part of the parent–child dynamic for generations. As parents it is our job to recognize that there are times when our kids are not ready to face certain risks or challenges until they reach a higher maturity level. We have to decide when they are ready to go to the park alone, ride their bike down the block, or drive to their first party. Today we are also faced with deciding when our children are old enough to have their first email account, to be on Twitter or Facebook, or to play M-rated video games.

Technology today creates new risks in an environment that many parents may not quite understand. It can seem frightening for parents who are unfamiliar with Facebook, gaming devices, or Club Penguin. Parenting today can be complicated and overwhelming, but keep in mind that being a good parent is about love, consistency, structure, and communication. It is important to be engaged, involved, and informed as a parent. It is important to keep the lines of communication open and to allow our children to grow and explore the world around them as their developmental and maturity levels allow. Being informed about technology can seem overwhelming, but it doesn't need to be. You are off to a good start. So relax; love your kids, provide common-sense boundaries, and keep the lines of communication open. Love and communication and consistent structure are the best tools we have to raise healthy and safe children.

Technology Terms

add-ons. Software made to work with another program; often created by third-party developers to "add" some new function or service. Often synonymous with "apps." For example, Adblock Plus (http://adblockplus.org) is an add-on for Firefox and Google Chrome web browsers and is useful for blocking website ads.

adware. Software that generates banner ads and popup ads on a computer. It is often hidden in and downloaded with freeware (which means the freeware is actually a Trojan horse), and consequently installed without the user's knowledge or permission.

AJAX. A group of programming technologies used for communication between a computer's operating system, often through the web browser, and a web server on the Internet. AJAX is an acronym referring to "Asynchronous JavaScript and XML."

apps. Software applications. Often synonymous with "add-ons." Typically used to describe third-party applications that can be installed on Facebook and other social networking sites. Apps are also available for iPads, smartphones, and other wireless devices.

avatar. Any icon that is used to represent a person online.

blog. Intended to describe any online website meant for users to record their opinions or ideas on a regular basis. Blogs can range from professional sites for reporters to personal sites for anyone with an opinion. Popular blog sites include Tumblr, Gawker, BuzzFeed, and *The Onion*. An abbreviation for "web log."

block. To prevent access; to obstruct. Most types of software or websites used for socializing come with the ability to block other members or prevent a user from being contacted by others.

bot. A general term for a "software robot." Apple's Siri voice-recognition software is a type of bot. Certain types of malware-infected computers are turned into bots and used by criminals to create a "bot-net." The criminal is called a "bot-herder" and uses the bot-net to engage in illegal activities such as denial of service (DOS) attacks or extortion.

buddy list (friend list). List of friends contained within a program used for communicating or socializing over the Internet. For example, Instant Message buddy list, Skype or Facebook friend list.

cache. A collection of Internet-related files stored in a directory (folder) on a user's computer. Each time you visit a website, some of the content of that web page is typically stored in your web browser's cache folder, making it faster and easier for the website page to load when you return to it. Cached files contain lots of information about the websites a person has visited. Web browsers, such as Internet Explorer or Safari, have settings that allow the user to limit files that are cached or allow the user to delete all cached files.

chat. A live text-based conversation between two or more people. Once considered possible only by using special chat software, today chat is possible between strangers on thousands of websites including many gaming sites, blogs, and other social media.

chat rooms. Specific online locations devoted to the opportunity for users to carry on text conversations.

clickstream. The collective recording of the clicking behavior of a user on the Internet or using Internet-related software. Clickstreams contain very valuable and sophisticated data for marketers and advertisers about users' online behavior.

Club Penguin. An online virtual world for children containing games, activities, and opportunities to socialize. Another way to think about Club Penguin is that it can be a social networking site for young children. Children choose a penguin to represent themselves in their virtual world.

cookie. A small amount of text that websites write onto your computer and that your computer sends back to the website the next time you visit it. Cookies only contain information; they are not computer programs and cannot behave like viruses or other malware. Among other things, cookies are used to keep track of your preferences or activities on a particular website. These are called "tracking cookies."

COPPA. An acronym for the Children's Online Privacy Protection Act (www.coppa.org) created by the Federal Trade Commission in 1998 to protect children from those United States companies online who wanted to collect their personal information without parental permission.

cramming. The practice of placing fraudulent or unauthorized charges on cell phone bills. Crammers often trick unsuspecting victims into clicking "OK" or "Submit" on web pages or cell phone spam (called "spim") that authorizes the charges to be made. Some children's game sites will periodically contain scam ads disguised as surveys and IQ quizzes that result in cramming charges.

cyberbully. Someone who bullies others online.

cyberbullying. Bullying behavior online. Due to the very diverse nature of online communication and interaction, many forms of cyberbullying are possible. See the Tools and Resources section at the end of this book for links to further information.

data aggregator. Persons or companies who collect data from a wide variety of online sources, including public records. The data is then generally resold to others.

denial of service (DOS) attack. An attack on a computer that prevents it from being available to others across the Internet. Generally, such attacks are meant to interrupt a service or server on the Internet. Bot-herders will sometimes direct a botnet to attack an Internet computer in this way for a variety of reasons. Sometimes it is done to extort money, and at other times it is done for political reasons.

DOM (document object model) storage. Methods for storing data in a web browser. For example, data about the visitor's web session or sessions over time.

drive-by download. A visitor's computer is infected with some form of malware the moment they arrive on a website. Computers without layers of software protection are more susceptible to a drive-by download. Windows-based computers are more susceptible than Apple computers.

Facebook. The most popular social networking site in the world; more than a billion account holders. Account holders in the United States are supposed to be at least 13 years old; however, millions of children under the age of 13 have accounts.

Facebook chat. A feature on Facebook in which members can have a real-time live text chat with their Facebook friends who are logged in.

firewall. Software that protects computers and routers from some types of Internet attacks and hacking.

Flash Player. Software made by Adobe and used to display commonly used animation and video on the Internet. Some scammers target their victims by tricking them into downloading a Trojan horse disguised as an updated flash player.

Formspring. A social website in which visitors are invited to interact anonymously with account holders. Due to the high level of bullying and harassment on the site, Children Online does not recommend that this website be used by children or teens.

freeware. Free software available on the Internet.

friend of a friend. Common term to describe anyone connected to a "friend." Keep in mind that in most cases, a friend of a friend may be a stranger or acquaintance.

friending/friended. To add someone to your list of online friends, thereby giving them access to your personal information and enabling them to interact with you online. An online friend can indeed be a real-life friend whom you already know. An online friend can be someone you once knew in person years ago and are now back in contact with. An online friend can be a friend of a friend, or simply an acquaintance or business contact who wants to know you better. However, in the case of thousands of teens, an online friend can be someone they have never met or had any connection with whatsoever, except for the friend request they received one day.

geolocation coordinates. A set of numbers that indicate an exact location on Earth. Geolocation coordinates are often embedded in digital photographs by a camera, and are accessible through smartphones, iPads, tablets, and other electronic devices. With this information it is possible to locate devices at any time or to identify the exact location of photos taken with digital cameras or uploaded from smartphone cameras.

Google Buzz. A social networking site created by Google that for a time was automatically included with every Gmail email account. Google Buzz was closed down in late 2011 as Google rolled out its new service: Google+.

Google+ (Plus). Google's social networking site debuted in mid-2011 and was meant to rival Facebook. Google+ is automatically given to anyone with a Gmail email account. Google+ offers "circles" of friends to help users control who sees their personal information.

hack. With regard to computers, hack means making an effort to break into something such as an online account, computer, or smartphone.

HD movies. High-definition movies "streamed" over the Internet.

iChat. An instant messaging software application created by Apple and included on all of its computers.

IMs. Abbreviation for "instant messages." Text messages sent using text messaging software such as AOL Instant Messanger (AIM), iChat, or the thousands of websites that support instant messaging. Even Skype is capable of sending IMs. Messages are text-based but may allow users to attach documents, photos, and links to the messages.

in-game currency. Currency used in association with a game played online or through a game console, such as Warcraft gold in *World of Warcraft*. In-game currency can be earned, traded for, or purchased with real money.

Instagram. A photo-sharing program and social network. Photos are shared between members and easily searched. Instagram has been a cause of concern for many parents because of the pornography available to all users.

instant messaging. The exchange of text messages in real-time. (See IMs)

iPad: Apple's popular tablet computer. Models can connect to the Internet like traditional computers and/or via cell phone networks.

iPod Touch. Apple computer's handheld device that plays music and videos, games, and downloadable applications. Newer models make video calls to other devices and accesses the Internet.; and records video. Includes Apple's popular FaceTime application.

iTunes. Software application made by Apple for both Macs and PCs to purchase, collect, store, and play music and videos (movies). iTunes comes installed on all Macs when purchased and is available for free for PCs (Windows operating systems).

JavaScript. A computer language often used for the Internet because of its ability to create interactive and dynamic content.

JPG (or JPEG). The file format (.jpg) that is typically used for computer and Internet photographs. "Jpegs" are capable of displaying thousands of colors. Jpegs can also be "doctored" to contain hidden malware or computer viruses.

malware. A general term for software harmful to computers or people's personal information stored on computers including cell phones. Both adware and spyware are types of malware.

mine personal data. The practice of collecting personal information.

mouse-over. When the mouse is moved over a link, every web browser and most email programs will display the real web address associated with that link in the lower left corner of the window. If the displayed link in the window is not to the expected website, then the link is a scam. Teach your child to be a careful reader! For example, *support.Faceebook.com* is not the same as *support.Facebook.com*.

MP3. A computer file format for music (sound) files universally understood and playable on all computers. MP3 files became popular because they manage to compress audio files (make them smaller) without much loss in quality *and* contain header information such as name of the song, artist, and album. MP3 files can also be "doctored" to contain hidden malware or computer viruses.

multiplayer gaming. Game playing on a website or using a gaming console, such as Wii, Xbox, or PlayStation, with many other players across the Internet in real time. Players can be friends in the same room or strangers across the world.

MySpace. A once-popular social networking site. Today, MySpace tends to be associated with musicians and music lovers. Like Facebook, MySpace enables users to socialize and post videos, audio files, and photographs to share with others. It is estimated that MySpace had more than 262 million users as of June 2012.

netizen. Citizen of the Internet.

news feed. On the social networking site Facebook, the News Feed is the list of updates from friends on their activities and posts. A user's News Feed is usually the column of information that they see upon logging into Facebook.

online friend. A person whom one knows online. It doesn't have to a friend in the traditional sense of the word. An online friend could be an acquaintance, a friend of a friend, or a complete stranger who simply sent a friend request.

online reputation. The opinions held about another person in large part due to their online activities, posts, and history. Generally speaking, there is far less privacy online that most people realize. It is very easy to search for information about someone to evaluate his online reputation. College admissions officers and potential employers have been known to search the online reputation of candidates they are evaluating.

parental control software. Software typically installed by parents to help them monitor their children's use of the Internet and/or cell phones. Parental control software is capable of allowing or denying specific categories of activities or websites as well as sending email reports to parents. Parents often feel that such software helps them set boundaries and restrictions in a virtual world where their children would otherwise have access to anything, and others have access to them.

PDF. A portable document format (.pdf) is a universal file format created by Adobe that is capable of being opened by all computers across the world. PDF files can contain text, graphics, photographs, and very sophisticated formatting. PDF files can also be used to transmit malware and cause computer infections.

phishing. A scammer's trick whereby the victim is tricked into visiting a fake website disguised to look like a legitimate site, such as Facebook, or a banking or credit card site. Phishing usually occurs through emails but can be perpetrated over the phone, via IM, or through Facebook. Once the victim attempts to log into the fake site, he has handed his login credentials over to the scammer. Some phishing sites are so sophisticated that the victim will actually be logged into the legitimate site after giving his credentials to the scammer and never suspect that anything is wrong. The scammers use their newly acquired account access for identity theft or to perpetrate fraud or theft.

PlayStation. A video game device produced by Sony. Most PlayStation games can be played in multiplayer mode over an Internet connection. Other generation PlayStations are called the PS2 and PS3. The portable players are called the PSP and the PS Vita.

post. To put up, as in "to post a reply on her Facebook Wall." Posting is generally thought of as displaying something in an online public place where others can see it.

privacy policy. The policies posted on websites that tell the users of the site how their personal information may and may not be used by the website owners. Keep in mind that most privacy policies contain a clause that states the privacy policy may be amended at any time by the website owner. In addition, some website owners have been found to do things they say they won't do in their privacy policy such as sell account holders' email addresses.

privacy settings. The settings for maintaining some aspect of privacy while using a website or Internet application. Some websites, like Facebook, have been known to change account holders' privacy settings when it makes changes to features in its website so that account holders' information is made publicly available.

private message. A message sent that is generally seen only by the intended recipient and therefore thought to be private. Though it is difficult to hack into private messages sent between account holders on Facebook, for example, it is common for private messages to be shown to others, forwarded, posted on a wall, or revealed by "over-the-shoulder" viewing or hacking into someone else's account.

profile. Software and websites designed for social interaction require an account holder to post publicly available information about himself. This information is called a profile. It may contain name, address, school, or work information. It may also contain selected quotes, things the account holder likes, whether or not he is in a relationship, and a photo. Profiles are generally searchable by anyone using the service or even by search engines. Profiles are part of all social networking sites, instant messaging software, Skype and iChat (video chat software), and many other websites. Cell phone numbers should never be posted in profiles because the numbers can easily be collected for cramming purposes.

ringtone. The tune or sound a cell phone makes when called. While cell phones contain many built-in ringtones, thousands more can be downloaded from the Internet. For some reason, scammers use the promise of "free ringtones" to attract and scam thousands of people around the world. Even searching Google for "free ringtones" can lead to a disproportionately high number of malware sites.

router. A device used to connect a home computer network to the Internet.

scammer. A person who swindles by means of deception or fraud.

screenshot. A picture or image made from all or a portion of a computer screen. The operating system of Apple computers have built-in screenshot capture capabilities. Holding "Command-Shift-3" together will create a screenshot of the entire screen, while "Command-Shift-4" will turn the cursor into crosshairs that can be dragged diagonally across the area to be captured. The screenshot then appears on the computer desktop. On a Windows-based computer, use the "Print Screen" button (sometimes labeled PrtSc or PrintScrn). To create a screenshot on an iPhone, hold down the Power button and the Home button at the same time. Your screenshot will appear in the camera roll of your photos.

screen time. The amount of time someone spends in front of electronic screens, including computers, TVs, tablets, and smartphones. A teen watching TV while logged into Facebook and texting would be considered to be using three screens at once.

Skype. A video chat application. Skype also has the ability to make Internet phone calls, instant message, share computer screens, and conduct video conference calls. Skype is available for Macs and PCs, and offers a free and paid service.

smartphone. A cell phone with many computer features that can access the Internet and use downloadable applications (apps). Most smartphones also contain built-in cameras and can access email and social networking sites such as Facebook.

social engineering. The art and business of manipulating people's behavior. For example, creating an email designed to frighten someone into clicking a link in the email or download a file attached to the email that results in a computer infection.

social network (social networking site, SNS). A website specifically designed for visitors to socialize with one another. SNSs typically enable users to share video, photos, audio files, chat, IM, and post things on each other's wall. Popular SNSs include Facebook, LinkedIn, MySpace, Twitter, Google+, DeviantART, Instagram, and LiveJournal. SNSs designed for younger children include Club Penguin, Webkinz, and Whyville. Even companies like McDonald's try to attract children by setting up their own social network sites (e.g., McWorld).

software bot. Software applications that run automated routines over the Internet. However, most people think of bots as computer infections that turn their personal computers into a bot controlled by criminals and used for illegal purposes.

spam. Unwanted and unsolicited electronic messages, often sent to users in bulk. Spam is most commonly sent via email but can be sent via IM, social networking sites, and texting. Spam that is sent via instant messaging is sometimes called "spim." Some spam is from legitimate sources but most of it is sent by criminals or criminal gangs.

spambot. A computer that has been turned into an automated sender of bulk spam. Some types of malware infections turn consumer's computers into spambots controlled by a bot-herder.

spammer. Someone who sends unwanted electronic messages in bulk.

spim. Spam sent via instant messaging.

spoofing. With regard to email, *spoofing* is the practice of altering any portion of an email such as the email address or source so that it appears to come from somewhere or someone it did not.

spyware. Malicious software secretly installed on a computer, usually via a Trojan horse strategy or during a drive-by download. Spyware captures information about the computer's users, such as logins, passwords, and other personal data useful for identity theft or financial gain.

tablets. A type of computer with a touch-sensitive screen that is generally flat, smaller, and more portable than a laptop. The most popular tablet computer is the Apple iPad. An example of a PC tablet is the Samsung Galaxy.

tagging. Adding names of people who appear in photos. Photos are typically tagged in social networking sites like Facebook or in photo storage sites like Flickr. Facebook's facial recognition software is so sophisticated that it will recognize faces and offer name suggestions based on friends connected to the account holder.

terms of service. The terms users must agree to in order to use a website. Terms of service are often long, written in "legalese," and can be changed at any time by the owners or managers of websites.

texting/text message. A text message sent via cell phone, generally, to another cell phone.

third-party application. Applications meant to be used with a primary application but created by a developer other than the developer of the primary application. Primary applications such as Facebook have thousands of other developers creating third-party applications to be used with Facebook. Most are legitimate, some are questionable, and some are disguised malware or are involved in data theft.

Timeline. On Facebook, Timeline is a service introduced in late 2011 that makes it possible for an account holder's friends to access all wall posts made on the account holder's wall since he joined Facebook. Timeline presents the account holder's history and other Facebook events such as status posts.

tracking. The act of gathering information about someone's Internet activity.

Trojan horse. A harmful program (malware) disguised to look like something desirable. For example, free downloadable games have been found to contain malware designed to give complete control over a consumer's computer to a criminal enterprise. Named after the ancient Trojan horse used to smuggle warriors behind the defenses of the city of Troy.

troll. Internet slang for someone who posts inflammatory remarks on a website.

Tumblr. A blogging web service that allows users to post text, videos, photos, and more on their web pages.

Twitter. A social networking service that allows account holders to send (and read) "tweets," which are text-based posts up to 140 characters in length. People often subscribe to follow celebrity tweets or friends' tweets.

upload. To send a file, such as a photo or Word document, from one's personal computer to a computer, server, or website located somewhere on the Internet.

video chat. To engage in a video conversation (audio and video exchange) with someone across the Internet. Skype and iChat software are designed specifically for video chat.

vlog (video blog). Same as a blog (see **blog**) but conducted through a live or recorded video session and posted on the Internet.

wall post. Putting a note, video, or photo on the part of a social networking site viewed by all of the account holder's friends. If the account is set to "friend of friend" or "public," then the post is seen by a much wider audience.

web browser. A software application used to access the Internet. Web browsers (and their manufacturers) include Internet Explorer (Microsoft), Chrome (Google), Safari (Apple), Firefox (Mozilla), and Opera (Opera Software).

web history. A record of websites visited and stored in a web browser's history settings. A browser's history can be retrieved going back several days unless it has been deleted by the user.

Webkinz. A commercial social networking site for younger children, in association with a purchased stuffed animal. The stuffed animal is transformed into a virtual "pet" online.

Wikipedia. A free online collaborative, multilingual encyclopedia that represents the collective wisdom of netizens who participate by contributing knowledge.

Xbox. A video game device produced by Microsoft. Most Xbox games can be played in multiplayer mode over an Internet connection. Types of Xbox devices include the Xbox Kinect and Xbox 360.

YouTube. One of the most popular websites on the planet, YouTube is a social networking site that enables member to post videos. Visitors can leave comments under any posted video (which explains why YouTube is rife with harassment.) Content ranges from "G" to "R." Children Online does not recommend YouTube for children under age 13.

zipped file. A zipped file (.zip) is a compressed computer file. Files are zipped to make them smaller and easier to send via email, for example. Zipped files can contain malware.

zombie flash cookie. A type of cookie (see **cookie**) that is stored in a computer directory associated with Adobe Flash. Flash cookies contain data about a user's web browsing activity and are capable of re-creating traditional cookies even after the traditional cookies have been deleted by the user. Hence the name "zombie" (as in coming back from the dead).

Tools and Resources

Tools and resources are arranged by topic. For a more extensive list of up-to-date resources, visit: www.ChildrenOnline.org/resources.html.

Cyberbullying and Online Harassment

Cyberbullying: Identification, Prevention and Response
Sameer Hinduja and Justin W. Patchin. 2010. Cyberbullying Research Center
    www.cyberbullying.us/Cyberbullying_Identification_Prevention_Response_
    Fact_Sheet.pdf

Internet Safety Project: Cyberbullying Research Center
    www.internetsafetyproject.org/wiki/cyberbullying-research-center

National Crime Prevention Council: Cyberbullying
    www.ncpc.org/topics/cyberbullying/

Face Bullying with Confidence: 8 Skills Kids Can Use Right Away
Irene van der Zande. Kidpower.org
    http://kidpower.org/library/article/prevent-bullying/?gclid=
    COqYxMf0oLECFcHb4AodlBZwWg

Economic Realities Online

Facebook Gets Religion for Revenue (economic realities of Facebook)
Geoffrey Fowler and Shayndi Rice. May 17, 2012. *Wall Street Journal*
    http://online.wsj.com/article/SB1000142405270230387960457774
    08481688851336.html

YouTube Ads Turn Videos Into Revenue
Claire Cain Miller. September 2, 2010. *New York Times*
    www.nytimes.com/2010/09/03/technology/03youtube.html

Online Ad Revenue Continues to Rise
Tanzina Vega. April 13, 2011. *New York Times*
    http://mediadecoder.blogs.nytimes.com/2011/04/13/
    online-ad-revenue-continues-to-rise/

Instant Messaging and Chat

Instant Messaging Tips
Common Sense Media. November 19, 2010
    www.commonsensemedia.org/advice-for-parents/instant-messaging-tips

Instant Message & Chat Room Safety Tips
Donna Rice Hughes. 2001. ProtectKids.com
    www.protectkids.com/parentsafety/imchatips.htm

Chat Room Safety
Larry Magid. SafeKids.com
    www.safekids.com/chat-room-safety/

Chat Room Safety Tips
ConnectSafely.org. Blog post on Education.com
    www.education.com/reference/article/chat-room-safety-tips-internet/

Facebook and Other Social Networking Sites

7.5 Million Facebook Users Are Below the Minimum Age
Leslie Horn. May 10, 2011. *PC Magazine*
    www.pcmag.com/article2/0,2817,2385122,00.asp

12 Things You Should Know About Facebook Timeline
Jill Duffy. January 25, 2012. *PC Magazine*
    www.pcmag.com/article2/0,2817,2393464,00.asp

The Complete Guide to Protecting Your Facebook Privacy When
Using Timeline (and the New Ticker)
Niall Harbison. April 16, 2012. Blog post on Simply Zesty
    www.simplyzesty.com/facebook/the-complete-guide-to-protecting-your-
    facebook-privacy-when-using-timeline-and-the-new-ticker/

A Parents' Guide to Facebook
Ann Coller and Larry Magid. Revised February 2012
   www.connectsafely.org/pdfs/fbparents.pdf

Facebook Privacy Concerns 2: Data Sharing Pitfalls and
Tweaking Privacy Settings
David B. April 12, 2012. Privacy PC
   http://privacy-pc.com/articles/facebook-privacy-concerns-2-data-sharing-
   pitfalls-and-tweaking-privacy-settings.html

How to Lock Down Your Facebook Account for Maximum Privacy and Security
Facecrooks.com. April 16, 2012
   http://facecrooks.com/Internet-Safety-Privacy/how-to-lockdown-your-face-
   book-account-for-maximum-privacy-and-security.html

Twitter Dictionary: A Guide to Understanding Twitter Lingo
Vangie Beal. Updated August 26, 2012. Webopedia
   www.webopedia.com/quick_ref/Twitter_Dictionary_Guide.asp

Internet Safety: 10 Safety Tips for Twitter Users
Tammy Blythe-Goodwin. September 2, 2010. SafetyWeb.com
   www.safetyweb.com/blog/internet-safety-10-safety-tips-for-twitter-users/

Internet Safety Project: Friendster (information and safety tips for Friendster)
   www.internetsafetyproject.org/wiki/friendster

Kids and Socializing Online (tips for helping kids socialize online)
OnGuardOnline.gov. September 2011
   http://onguardonline.gov/articles/0012-kids-and-socializing-online

Gaming

ESRB Ratings Guide (understanding video game ratings)
Entertainment Software Rating Board (ESRB)
   www.esrb.org/ratings/ratings_guide.jsp

How the ESRB Works (how ratings work and what they mean)
Ed Grabianowski. How Stuff Works
   http://electronics.howstuffworks.com/esrb.htm

Common Sense Media Guide to Games
www.commonsensemedia.org/search/video%20games

Healthy Habits for TV, Video Games, and the Internet
Mary Gavin, MD. March 2011. KidsHealth.org
http://kidshealth.org/parent/positive/family/tv_habits.html

Parental Control Software

Action Alert: Protecting Kids from Online Dangers
www.actionalert.com

iNet Safety Bubble for Mobile Devices
www.inetsafetybubble.com

Kaspersky Parental Controls (for the iPad, iPhone, Android smartphone,
and tablets)
http://usa.kaspersky.com/products-services/home-computer-security/
parental-control

K9 Web Protection Browser (for the iPhone, iPad, and iPod Touch)
http://itunes.apple.com/us/app/k9-web-protection-browser/id407657840?mt=8

Instructions for the K9 Web Protection Browser: Settings for iPhone, iPod, iPad
www1.k9webprotection.com/support/set-idevice-restrictions

Mobicip: Safe and Secure Mobile Internet
www.mobicip.com

Privacy

Data Mining: How Companies Now Know Everything about You
Joel Stein. March 10, 2011. *Time*
www.time.com/time/magazine/article/0,9171,2058205,00.html

Facebook, Instagram, and Your Privacy
Vanessa Clark. April 11, 2012. Mobiflock.com
www.mobiflock.com/for-me/facebook-instagram-and-your-privacy

How to Muddy Your Tracks on the Internet
Kate Murphy. May 2, 2012. *New York Times*
www.nytimes.com/2012/05/03/technology/personaltech/how-to-muddy-your-tracks-on-the-internet.html

Scams, Tricks, and Computer Threats

Anti-Phishing Working Group (APWG)
www.antiphishing.org

Phishing.org
www.phishing.org

Federal Bureau of Investigation (FBI) site for Cyber Crime
www.fbi.gov/about-us/investigate/cyber/cyber

Report Fraud (government site for reporting computer fraud)
www.stopfraud.gov/report.html

Sites for Children and Teens

Kids-Online.com: Kid Chat (safe chat space for children and teens)
www.kids-online.com

PBS Kids
http://pbskids.org

Funbrain (games/puzzles)
www.funbrain.com

Exploratorium (science-related activities, videos, and links)
www.exploratorium.edu

Meet Me at the Corner (a safe YouTube alternative)
www.meetmeatthecorner.org

Technology and Children/Teens

Five Ways to Keep Technology from Ruining Your Kids
Amy Henry. March 6, 2012. Blog post at Patheos
www.patheos.com/blogs/whatshesaid/2012/03/
five-ways-to-keep-technology-from-ruining-your-kids

Is the Internet Hurting Children?
Chelsea Clinton and James Steyer. Updated May 21, 2012. CNN Opinion
www.cnn.com/2012/05/21/opinion/clinton-steyer-internet-kids/index.
html?hpt=hp_c3

Study: Multitasking Hinders Youth Social Skills
Mark Millian. January 25, 2012. CNN Tech
www.cnn.com/2012/01/25/tech/social-media/multitasking-kids/index.
html?hpt=hp_c3

Study: Face Time Benefits Preteens
Rachel Emma Silverman. January 30, 2012. *Wall Street Journal*
http://blogs.wsj.com/juggle/2012/01/30/study-face-time-benefits-preteens/

Time Management Software

EZ Internet Timer (for PCs)
www.internettimer.net

Rescue Time (time management tracking software)
www.rescuetime.com

SelfControl (for Mac OS X; blocks access to mail servers and websites for
a set period of time)
http://visitsteve.com/made/selfcontrol/

Time Controls for the Internet (from McAfee)
www.internetsafety.com/manage-internet-access-time.php